5-Ingredient Slow Cooker Recipes

Jean Paré

www.companyscoming.com
visit our website

Front Cover

Florentine Chicken
Lasagna, page 75

Back Cover

1. Texas Chili, page 59
2. Steak and Veggie Dinner,
   page 70
3. Tender Beef With Lemon
   Parsley, page 64

5-Ingredient Slow Cooker Recipes

Third Printing March 2010

Library and Archives Canada Cataloguing in Publication
Paré, Jean, date-
5 ingredient slow cooker recipes / Jean Paré.
(Original series) Includes index.
ISBN 978-1-897477-06-9
1. Electric cookery, Slow.   I. Title.
II. Title: Five ingredient slow cooker recipes.
TX827.P366 2009   641.5'884   C2009-900799-1

Published by
Company's Coming Publishing Limited
2311 – 96 Street
Edmonton, Alberta, Canada T6N 1G3
Tel: 780-450-6223   Fax: 780-450-1857
www.companyscoming.com

Company's Coming is a registered trademark owned by Company's Coming Publishing Limited

We acknowledge the financial support of the Government of Canada through the Book Publishing Industry Development Program (BPIDP) for our publishing activities.

Printed in China

We gratefully acknowledge the following suppliers for their generous support of our Test and Photography Kitchens:

Broil King Barbecues
Corelle®
Hamilton Beach® Canada
Lagostina®
Proctor Silex® Canada
Tupperware®

Our special thanks to the following businesses for providing props for photography:

Cherison Enterprises
Emile Henry
Out of the Fire Studio
Stokes

Get more great recipes...FREE!

click

search

print

cook

From apple pie to zucchini bread, we've got you covered. Browse our free online recipes for Guaranteed Great!™ results.

You can also sign up to receive our **FREE online newsletter**. You'll receive exclusive offers, FREE recipes & cooking tips, new title previews, and much more...all delivered to your in-box.

So don't delay, visit our website today!

www.companyscoming.com
visit our ↖ website

Company's Coming Cookbooks

Quick & easy recipes; everyday ingredients!

Original Series

- Softcover, 160 pages
- Lay-flat plastic comb binding
- Full-colour photos
- Nutrition information

Original Series

- Softcover, 160 pages
- Lay-flat plastic comb binding
- Full-colour photos
- Nutrition information

3-in-1 Cookcook Collection

- Softcover, 208 pages
- Lay-flat plastic coil binding
- Full-colour photos

Special Occasion Series

- Softcover, 176 pages
- Full-colour photos
- Nutrition information

For a complete listing of our cookbooks, visit our website:
www.companyscoming.com

Table of Contents

Beverages

Soups

Main Courses

Beef

Chicken & Turkey

Pork & Lamb

Vegetarian

Desserts

The Company's Coming Story

Jean Paré (pronounced "jeen PAIR-ee") grew up understanding that the combination of family, friends and home cooking is the best recipe for a good life. From her mother, she learned to appreciate good cooking, while her father praised even her earliest attempts in the kitchen. When Jean left home, she took with her a love of cooking, many family recipes and an intriguing desire to read cookbooks as if they were novels!

"Never share a recipe you wouldn't use yourself."

When her four children had all reached school age, Jean volunteered to cater the 50th anniversary celebration of the Vermilion School of Agriculture, now Lakeland College, in Alberta, Canada. Working out of her home, Jean prepared a dinner for more than 1,000 people, launching a flourishing catering operation that continued for over 18 years. During that time, she had countless opportunities to test new ideas with immediate feedback—resulting in empty plates and contented customers! Whether preparing cocktail sandwiches for a house party or serving a hot meal for 1,500 people, Jean Paré earned a reputation for great food, courteous service and reasonable prices.

As requests for her recipes increased, Jean was often asked the question, "Why don't you write a cookbook?" Jean responded by teaming up with her son, Grant Lovig, in the fall of 1980 to form Company's Coming Publishing Limited. The publication of *150 Delicious Squares* on April 14, 1981 marked the debut of what would soon become one of the world's most popular cookbook series.

The company has grown since those early days when Jean worked from a spare bedroom in her home. Today, she continues to write recipes while working closely with the staff of the Recipe Factory, as the Company's Coming test kitchen is affectionately known.

There she fills the role of mentor, assisting with the development of recipes people most want to use for everyday cooking and easy entertaining. Every Company's Coming recipe is *kitchen-tested* before it is approved for publication.

Jean's daughter, Gail Lovig, is responsible for marketing and distribution, leading a team that includes sales personnel located in major cities across Canada. Company's Coming cookbooks are distributed in Canada, the United States, Australia and other world markets. Bestsellers many times over in English, Company's Coming cookbooks have also been published in French and Spanish.

Familiar and trusted in home kitchens around the world, Company's Coming cookbooks are offered in a variety of formats. Highly regarded as kitchen workbooks, the softcover Original Series, with its lay-flat plastic comb binding, is still a favourite among readers.

Jean Paré's approach to cooking has always called for *quick and easy recipes* using *everyday ingredients*. That view has served her well. The recipient of many awards, including the Queen Elizabeth Golden Jubilee Medal, Jean was appointed Member of the Order of Canada, her country's highest lifetime achievement honour.

Jean continues to gain new supporters by adhering to what she calls The Golden Rule of Cooking: *Never share a recipe you wouldn't use yourself.* It's an approach that has worked—*millions of times over!*

Foreword

Life can get so hectic for busy people and families. Too often it becomes tempting to stop for fast food or call for takeout instead of making dinner. Eating this way is fine as an occasional treat, but if we do it too often, it can end up just shrinking our wallets and expanding our waistlines. Luckily, the solution to this dinner-time dilemma can be found in your very own kitchen: the slow cooker.

Slow-cooker cooking is convenient and economical, and by rustling up just a few simple ingredients, you can make a delicious, filling meal for your family every night—and you don't even have to be in the kitchen to do it! *5-Ingredient Slow Cooker Recipes* is packed with great ideas to make cooking dinner—and plenty more—a snap every day of the week. All the recipes feature just five ingredients, including quality convenience products, to keep prep time short and low-fuss. Simply mix everything together in your slow cooker in the morning, then set it and forget it. A tasty, home-cooked dinner will be ready and waiting for you by supper time!

But why limit yourself to weekday dinners? Try serving Sugar and Spice Pecans or Garlic Mushrooms at your next party. Hot Mulled Cider and Hazelnut Hot Chocolate will warm you up on those cold winter evenings. Or indulge yourself a little with Chocolate Hazelnut Cheesecake or Coconut Rice Pudding, for those times when your sweet tooth needs satisfying.

We've taken advantage of readily available convenience products to save you time and effort. Ingredients run from the everyday, such as frozen meatballs, canned tomatoes and condensed soup mixes, to the more exotic, like grape leaves, sambal oelek, okra and quinoa. As usual, we've come up with delicious, kitchen-tested combinations that will make your five-ingredient dishes a hit with family and friends.

With *5-Ingredient Slow Cooker Recipes,* you'll be able to prepare satisfying, nourishing meals using simple ingredients and minimal effort. Cooking was never so easy—or delicious!

Jean Paré

Nutrition Information Guidelines

Each recipe is analyzed using the most current version of the Canadian Nutrient File from Health Canada, which is based on the United States Department of Agriculture (USDA) Nutrient Database.

- If more than one ingredient is listed (such as "butter or hard margarine"), or if a range is given (1 – 2 tsp., 5 – 10 mL), only the first ingredient or first amount is analyzed.

- For meat, poultry and fish, the serving size per person is based on the recommended 4 oz. (113 g) uncooked weight (without bone), which is 2 – 3 oz. (57 – 85 g) cooked weight (without bone)—approximately the size of a deck of playing cards.

- Milk used is 1% M.F. (milk fat), unless otherwise stated.

- Cooking oil used is canola oil, unless otherwise stated.

- Ingredients indicating "sprinkle," "optional," or "for garnish" are not included in the nutrition information.

- The fat in recipes and combination foods can vary greatly depending on the sources and types of fats used in each specific ingredient. For these reasons, the amount of saturated, monounsaturated and polyunsaturated fats may not add up to the total fat content.

Vera C. Mazurak, Ph.D.
Nutritionist

Slow Cooker Basics

A slow cooker can be a versatile tool in your kitchen. Besides being a great way to prepare a variety of dishes, it can serve as an extra pot any time you cook; it won't heat up your kitchen and it won't dry out your food the way your oven might. Slow cooking also allows you to prepare more economical cuts of meat, leaving them moist and tender.

To save you time, we've limited our recipes to just five ingredients, and focused on those that add the most flavour. A few ingredients are not listed because we felt that they are integral to the cooking process and don't need to be counted: salt and pepper, water for cooking pasta and oil for greasing a frying pan, for example. In recipes using the zest and juice of citrus fruits, the two are considered part of the same ingredient and are not listed individually.

Our recipes have been written to represent the most common sizes of slow cookers on the market, and each recipe has been tested to ensure great results. You may need to increase or decrease a recipe to fit your particular slow cooker. Consult your owner's manual for particular guidelines.

In addition to the specific cooking tips included in the recipes, we also offer these general guidelines, which you can apply any time you use your slow cooker:

- Cooking times can vary with different makes and models of slow cookers, and some cookers can be forgiving if you go over the specified time in the recipe. However, for best results, follow the cooking times provided in our recipes, as they have all been thoroughly tested.

- Fill your slow cooker at least halfway, but no more than three-quarters full, for the most even heat distribution. (Ingredients will typically cook down in volume.) Note that some of our recipes, such as dips, deviate from this general principle because we are simply *heating* the ingredients, not *cooking* them. We've tested the recipes to make sure they work, but if you happen to have a smaller slow cooker—such as a 1 1/2 quart (1.5 L) size—it would work well.

- When using your slow cooker to heat dips, transfer the warmed dip to a fondue pot, on lowest heat, for a more pleasing presentation.

- Thaw frozen food before cooking to ensure accurate cooking times.

- Don't lift the lid while food is cooking because heat and moisture will escape, adding 20 to 30 extra minutes of cooking time to the recipe each time the lid is raised.

- Layer foods in this order for best results: root vegetables (carrots, onions, beets, potatoes) at the bottom, then meats, seasonings and, lastly, non-root vegetables (beans, peas, corn). Generally, the ingredients that take longest to cook should be at the bottom, and those that cook most quickly should be near the top.

- To adapt one of your own recipes for a slow cooker, you may have to reduce the liquid in the recipe by up to 50 per cent and add more herbs and spices. Slow cooking foods at a lower temperature can produce a fair amount of liquid, which dilutes the herbs or spices that enhance flavour.

- Use dried herbs while the dish is cooking, and add fresh herbs to the pot in the final moments, or just before serving for an extra dash of flavour.

- Trim meat of all visible fat before adding it to the slow cooker.

- Pre-brown meat and ingredients such as onions and garlic to add a more robust flavour and colour to a dish.

If you've never used a slow cooker before, these safety tips should ensure safe cooking:

- Always cook large pieces of meat such as roasts on High, unless they have been pre-browned first, to get the temperature up more quickly and into a safe zone.

- Keep ingredients, especially raw meat, refrigerated and in separate containers until you are ready to assemble the recipe.

- Partially cooking meat and refrigerating it can lead to bacterial growth. Our make-ahead instructions keep food safety in mind, so follow them as they are written.

- Test the doneness of large pieces of meat with a thermometer to ensure the correct temperature has been reached.

- Don't reheat leftover food in a slow cooker because it doesn't reach the necessary high temperature quickly enough to eliminate potential bacterial growth.

- Chill all cooked food within two hours of cooking.

Get to Know Your Slow Cooker

In addition to the advice we've provided on these pages, it's a good idea to read through the instruction manual that came with your slow cooker. It will outline how to get the most from your particular brand of cooker, how cooking times can vary between different brands and how high altitude and power fluctuations can affect your slow cooker. Once you've read the manual and prepared a few meals, you'll get to know your slow cooker well enough to anticipate how it will respond to any given recipe.

A slow cooker uses only a small amount of electricity, making slow cooking a cost-effective way to cook. Because the heating coils are on the sides rather than the bottom of the cooker, food is not likely to burn or dry out. With *5-Ingredient Slow Cooker Recipes*, you'll be able to maximize the value of your appliance by using it to prepare not just traditional soups and stews, but a wide array of appetizers, beverages and desserts as well. The possibilities truly are endless!

Lemony Vine Leaves

These Greek-style grape leaves are a great summertime appetizer to serve with tzatziki dip.

Long-grain white rice	2 cups	500 mL
Roasted red pepper cream cheese	1 cup	250 mL
Greek seasoning	2 tbsp.	30 mL
Grape leaves, rinsed and drained, tough stems removed	60	60
Lemon juice	1/3 cup	75 mL

Mix first 3 ingredients and a sprinkle of salt and pepper in medium bowl until no dry rice remains.

Arrange 38 to 40 grape leaves on work surface, vein-side up, stem end closest to you. Spoon about 1 tbsp. (15 mL) rice mixture onto leaf about 1/2 inch (12 mm) from stem end of leaf. Fold bottom of leaf over rice mixture. Fold in sides. Roll up from bottom to enclose filling (see Note 1). Repeat with remaining leaves and rice mixture. Cover bottom of greased 3 1/2 to 4 quart (3.5 to 4 L) slow cooker with 4 to 5 grape leaves. Arrange rolls, seam-side down, close together in single layer over leaves. Cover with 4 to 5 grape leaves. Repeat with remaining rolls and leaves.

Add lemon juice and 4 cups (1 L) water. Do not stir. Place a heatproof plate on top to keep rolls submerged during cooking (see Note 2). Cook, covered, on Low for 7 to 8 hours or on High for 3 1/2 to 4 hours until rice is tender. Let stand, covered, for 20 minutes. Makes 38 to 40 stuffed grape leaves.

1 stuffed grape leaf: 57 Calories; 1.6 g Total Fat (trace Mono, 0.1 g Poly, 1.0 g Sat); 6 mg Cholesterol; 9 g Carbohydrate; trace Fibre; 1 g Protein; 44 mg Sodium

Note 1: Leaves should be rolled securely, but not too tightly, as the filling will expand during cooking.

Note 2: If you have an oval slow cooker that will not fit a round plate, use two smaller, heatproof plates that will fit.

Variation: Try them with herb and garlic cream cheese in place of the red pepper cream cheese.

Sugar and Spice Pecans

These sweet, toasted treats won't stay in the candy dish for long.

Pecan halves	4 cups	1 L
Butter	1/3 cup	75 mL
Brown sugar, packed	1/2 cup	125 mL
Ground cinnamon	1 1/2 tsp.	7 mL
Ground allspice	1/4 tsp.	1 mL

Put pecans into 3 1/2 to 4 quart (3.5 to 4 L) slow cooker.

Stir butter and sugar in small saucepan on medium until butter is melted. Stir. Pour over pecans. Stir until coated. Cook, covered, on High for 30 minutes. Stir. Reduce heat to Low. Cook, covered, for about 2 hours, stirring every 30 minutes, until pecans are glazed and golden.

Combine cinnamon and allspice in small cup. Sprinkle over nuts. Stir. Spread evenly on ungreased baking sheet to cool. Makes about 4 cups (1 L).

1/4 cup (60 mL): 247 Calories; 23.2 g Total Fat (12.0 g Mono, 6.0 g Poly, 4.1 g Sat); 10 mg Cholesterol; 11 g Carbohydrate; 3 g Fibre; 3 g Protein; 30 mg Sodium

Nacho Cheese Fondue

This Mexican-themed cheese fondue will be devoured by hungry kids, teenagers and adults alike! Serve with cubed bread or tortilla chips straight from the slow cooker on the lowest setting, or transfer to a serving bowl.

Process cheese spread	2 cups	500 mL
Roasted red pepper cream cheese	1 cup	250 mL
Salsa	1 cup	250 mL
Finely chopped red pepper	1/2 cup	125 mL
Can of diced green chilies	4 oz.	113 g

Combine all 5 ingredients in 3 1/2 to 4 quart (3.5 to 4 L) slow cooker. Cook, covered, on Low for 2 to 3 hours or on High for 1 to 1 1/2 hours until heated through. Makes about 5 cups (1.25 L).

1/4 cup (60 mL): 106 Calories; 8.4 g Total Fat (0 g Mono, trace Poly, 4.2 g Sat); 28 mg Cholesterol; 4 g Carbohydrate; trace Fibre; 4 g Protein; 291 mg Sodium

Baba Ganoush

Cooking up this exotic favourite doesn't get any easier than with the slow cooker. Try it hot or cold and serve with fresh pita or pita chips.

Chopped, peeled Asian eggplant	5 cups	1.25 L
Garlic cloves, minced	2	2
Ground cumin	1 tsp.	5 mL
Olive oil, divided	3 tbsp.	50 mL
Lemon juice	1 tbsp.	15 mL

Combine first 3 ingredients, 2 tbsp. (30 mL) olive oil, 1/4 cup (60 mL) water and a generous sprinkle of salt and pepper in 3 1/2 to 4 quart (3.5 to 4 L) slow cooker. Cook, covered, on Low for 4 to 6 hours or on High for 2 to 3 hours, stirring once at halftime, until soft and fragrant.

Transfer to blender or food processor. Add lemon juice and remaining olive oil. Process until smooth (see Safety Tip). Makes about 1 3/4 cups (425 mL).

1/3 cup (75 mL): 88 Calories; 7.9 g Total Fat (5.5 g Mono, 1.2 g Poly, 1.1 g Sat); 0 mg Cholesterol; 5 g Carbohydrate; 3 g Fibre; 1 g Protein; 214 mg Sodium

Pictured on page 17.

Safety Tip: Follow manufacturer's instructions for processing hot liquids.

Creamy Seafood Filling

When you're in the mood to indulge, this elegant, delicious lobster and seafood appetizer is just the ticket. Serve over fresh puff pastry cups or points and garnish with sprigs of fresh dill.

Chive and onion cream cheese	2 cups	500 mL
Can of frozen lobster meat, thawed, drained, larger pieces cut up	11 1/3 oz.	320 g
Dry (or alcohol-free) white wine	1/3 cup	75 mL
Shrimp and scallop medley, thawed, drained and blotted dry	1 lb.	454 g
Chopped fresh dill (or 1/2 tsp., 2 mL, dried)	2 tsp.	10 mL

(continued on next page)

Combine first 3 ingredients and a sprinkle of pepper in 3 1/2 to 4 quart (3.5 to 4 L) slow cooker. Cook, covered, on Low for 3 to 4 hours or on High for 1 1/2 to 2 hours. Stir until smooth.

Add shrimp and scallops. Stir. Cook, covered, on High for about 20 minutes until shrimp turn pink.

Add dill. Stir. Makes about 4 cups (1 L).

1/4 cup (60 mL): 168 Calories; 10.7 g Total Fat (0.1 g Mono, 0.3 g Poly, 7.1 g Sat); 72 mg Cholesterol; 3 g Carbohydrate; trace Fibre; 11 g Protein; 220 mg Sodium

---

Pork and Guacamole Tostadas

Serve this easy, crowd-pleasing appetizer at your next party. About half of the pork mixture will be left over—it can be frozen or made into fajitas for lunch!

Boneless pork shoulder butt roast, trimmed of fat	2 lbs.	900 g
Hot salsa	2 cups	500 mL
Tortilla chips	9 oz.	250 g
Prepared guacamole	1 1/2 cups	375 mL
Grated jalapeño Monterey Jack cheese	1 1/2 cups	375 mL

Place roast in 3 1/2 to 4 quart (3.5 to 4 L) slow cooker. Sprinkle with salt and pepper. Pour 1 1/2 cups (375 mL) salsa over top. Cook, covered, on High for 4 1/2 to 5 hours. Transfer roast to large plate. Skim and discard fat from sauce. Shred pork with 2 forks. Return to sauce. Add remaining salsa. Stir.

Spoon pork mixture over each tortilla chip. Top with guacamole. Sprinkle with cheese. Makes 48 tostadas.

1 tostada: 79 Calories; 4.4 g Total Fat (0.8 g Mono, 0.2 g Poly, 1.4 g Sat); 14 mg Cholesterol; 5 g Carbohydrate; 1 g Fibre; 5 g Protein; 155 mg Sodium

Pictured on page 71.

Garlic Mushrooms

Enjoy these creamy, flavourful mushrooms with crostini or baguette slices—or try serving them alongside a steak dinner!

Fresh small white mushrooms	2 lbs.	900 g
Alfredo pasta sauce	1/2 cup	125 mL
Dry (or alcohol-free) white wine	1/4 cup	60 mL
Garlic cloves, minced	4	4
(or 1 tsp., 5 ml, powder)		
Lemon juice	2 tsp.	10 mL

Arrange mushrooms on large greased baking sheet with sides. Broil on top rack in oven for about 15 minutes, stirring once, until starting to brown. Drain and discard any liquid. Transfer to 3 1/2 to 4 quart (3.5 to 4 L) slow cooker.

Add next 3 ingredients and a sprinkle of pepper. Stir. Cook, covered, on Low for 5 to 6 hours or on High for 2 1/2 to 3 hours.

Add lemon juice. Stir. Makes about 3 cups (750 mL).

1/3 cup (75 mL): 54 Calories; 2.4 g Total Fat (0 g Mono, 0 g Poly, 0.8 g Sat); 6 mg Cholesterol; 5 g Carbohydrate; trace Fibre; 2 g Protein; 83 mg Sodium

White Bean and Garlic Spread

For garlic lovers! Spread over crostini slices or melba toast. One clove can be left out if you prefer a milder garlic flavour.

Dried navy beans	1 1/2 cups	375 mL
Italian seasoning	2 tbsp.	30 mL
Large lemon	1	1
Olive oil	2 tbsp.	30 mL
Garlic cloves, minced (or 1/2 tsp.,	2	2
2 mL, powder)		

Put beans into medium bowl. Add water until 2 inches (5 cm) above beans. Let stand overnight (see Tip, page 15). Drain. Rinse beans. Drain. Transfer to 3 1/2 to 4 quart (3.5 to 4 L) slow cooker.

(continued on next page)

Add Italian seasoning and 3 cups (750 mL) water. Cook, covered, on High for 3 1/2 to 4 hours until beans are tender (see Note). Drain, reserving 1/4 cup (60 mL) cooking liquid. Transfer beans and liquid to food processor.

Grate 1 tsp. (5 mL) lemon zest into bean mixture. Squeeze in 2 tbsp. (30 mL) lemon juice. Add olive oil, garlic and a generous sprinkle of salt and pepper. Carefully process until smooth (see Safety Tip). Makes about 3 1/2 cups (875 mL).

1/3 cup (75 mL): 67 Calories; 2.8 g Total Fat (1.9 g Mono, 0.5 g Poly, 0.4 g Sat); 0 mg Cholesterol; 8 g Carbohydrate; 2 g Fibre; 3 g Protein; 279 mg Sodium

Safety Tip: Follow manufacturer's instructions for processing hot liquids.

Note: Cooking this spread on Low is not recommended, as it may not fully cook the beans.

Spiced Granola

For a personal touch, add your favourite dried fruits, toasted nuts or seeds after the granola cools. Pour in some milk or stir it up with yogurt for a nutritious breakfast.

Brown sugar, packed	1/4 cup	60 mL
Cooking oil	1/4 cup	60 mL
Liquid honey	1/4 cup	60 mL
Pumpkin pie spice	1/4 tsp.	1 mL
Large flake rolled oats	5 cups	1.25 L

Combine first 4 ingredients in 3 1/2 to 4 quart (3.5 to 4 L) slow cooker.

Add oats. Stir until coated. Lay double layer of tea towels over slow cooker liner. Cover with lid. Cook on High for 1 hour. Stir. Lay double layer of tea towel over slow cooker liner. Cover with lid. Cook on Low for about 30 minutes until golden. Spread evenly on ungreased baking sheet to cool and crisp. Makes about 5 cups (1.25 L).

1/2 cup (125 mL): 263 Calories; 8.6 g Total Fat (3.2 g Mono, 1.6 g Poly, 0.4 g Sat); 0 mg Cholesterol; 41 g Carbohydrate; 5 g Fibre; 6 g Protein; 2 mg Sodium

 tip If you would like a quicker method for soaking the beans, place beans in a heatproof dish, cover with boiling water and let stand for at least one hour until cool.

Artichoke Spinach Dip

Lovely wine and pesto flavours give this rich dip a real bistro feel—it tastes fabulous served with fresh baguette slices.

Jar of marinated artichoke hearts, drained and chopped	12 oz.	340 mL
Herb and garlic cream cheese	1 cup	250 mL
Dry (or alcohol-free) white wine	1/2 cup	125 mL
Coarsely chopped fresh spinach leaves, lightly packed	4 cups	1 L
Basil pesto	1/4 cup	60 mL

Combine first 3 ingredients and a sprinkle of pepper in 3 1/2 to 4 quart (3.5 to 4 L) slow cooker. Cook, covered, on Low for 4 to 5 hours or on High for 2 to 2 1/2 hours. Stir until smooth.

Add spinach and pesto. Stir. Makes about 2 1/2 cups (625 mL).

1/4 cup (60 mL): 113 Calories; 8.8 g Total Fat (0 g Mono, trace Poly, 4.1 g Sat); 26 mg Cholesterol; 4 g Carbohydrate; trace Fibre; 3 g Protein; 256 mg Sodium

Pictured at right.

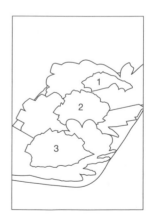

1. Baba Ganoush, page 12
2. Hot Crab Dip, page 22
3. Artichoke Spinach Dip, above

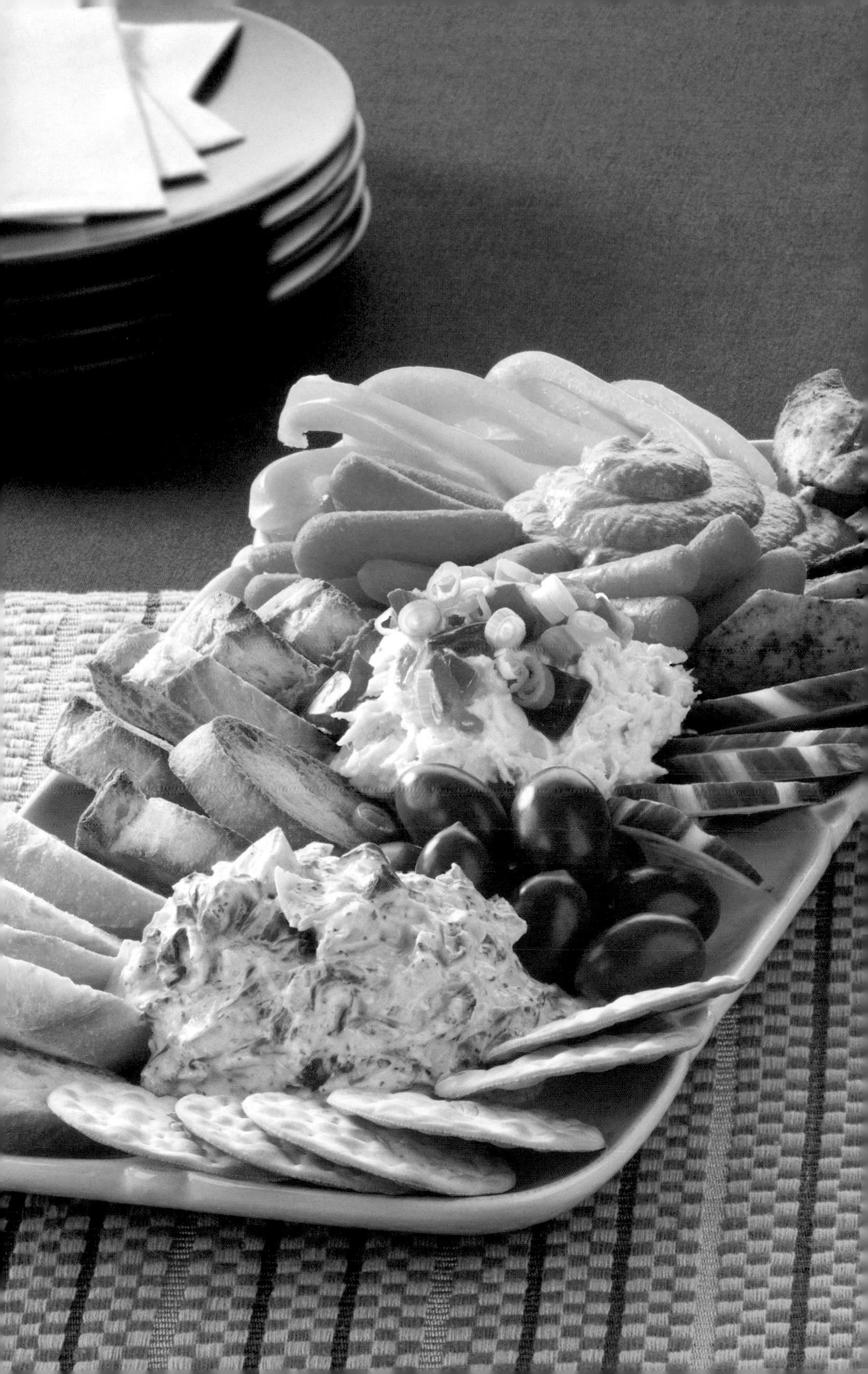

Honey Garlic Wings

These tender wings are a real crowd-pleaser with their classic honey garlic flavour. Set them out hot on a platter and watch everyone gather 'round.

Split chicken wings, tips discarded	3 lbs.	1.4 kg
Liquid honey	1 cup	250 mL
Soy sauce	1/2 cup	125 mL
Garlic cloves, minced	2	2
(or 1/2 tsp., 2 mL, powder)		
Ground ginger	1/4 tsp.	1 mL

Arrange wings on greased baking sheet with sides. Sprinkle with pepper. Broil on top rack in oven for about 6 minutes per side until browned. Transfer to 4 to 5 quart (4 to 5 L) slow cooker.

Combine remaining 4 ingredients in small bowl. Pour over chicken. Stir until coated. Cook, covered, on Low for 4 to 5 hours or on High for 2 to 2 1/2 hours. Discard liquid from slow cooker. Makes about 32 wings.

1 wing: 114 Calories; 6.7 g Total Fat (0 g Mono, 0 g Poly, 1.8 g Sat); 32 mg Cholesterol; 5 g Carbohydrate; trace Fibre; 8 g Protein; 196 mg Sodium

1. Mulled Blackcurrant Sipper, page 29
2. Warm and Fuzzy Navel, page 27
3. Hot Fruit Punch, page 30

Spicy Black-Eyed Pea Dip

This hot and spicy dip may be topped with chopped green onion and grated Monterey Jack cheese. It's perfect for dipping fresh vegetables or spooning onto slices of ciabatta bread or taco chips. Serve warm from the slow cooker, as it will thicken as it cools.

Cans of black-eyed peas (19 oz., 540 mL, each), rinsed and drained	2	2
Process cheese loaf, chopped	16 oz.	450 g
Hot chunky salsa	1 cup	250 mL
Taco seasoning mix, stir before measuring	1 tbsp.	15 mL
Canned sliced jalapeño peppers, finely chopped	2 tsp.	10 mL

Combine all 5 ingredients in 3 1/2 to 4 quart (3.5 to 4 L) slow cooker. Cook, covered, on Low for 2 to 3 hours or on High for 1 to 1 1/2 hours, stirring twice, until heated through. Break up mixture with potato masher. Makes about 5 cups (1.25 L).

1/4 cup (60 mL): 100 Calories; 4.8 g Total Fat (0 g Mono, 0 g Poly, 3.2 g Sat); 16 mg Cholesterol; 10 g Carbohydrate; 2 g Fibre; 6 g Protein; 703 mg Sodium

Chili Snack Mix

This crunchy treat balances sweet and spicy flavours, and is great for all ages. It will disappear fast when snack time arrives!

"O"-shaped toasted oat cereal	2 cups	500 mL
Small pretzels	2 cups	500 mL
Butter (or hard margarine), melted	1/4 cup	60 mL
Chili seasoning mix, stir before measuring	2 tbsp.	30 mL
Trail mix	2 cups	500 mL

Combine first 4 ingredients in 3 1/2 to 4 quart (3.5 to 4 L) slow cooker. Cook, covered, on High for 30 minutes. Stir. Cook, covered, on Low for 1 to 1 1/2 hours, stirring every 20 minutes, until crisp and golden. Spread on ungreased baking sheet to cool. Transfer to large bowl.

(continued on next page)

Add trail mix. Stir. Makes about 6 cups (1.5 L).

1/3 cup (75 mL): 133 Calories; 7.9 g Total Fat (2.9 g Mono, 1.8 g Poly, 2.6 g Sat); 7 mg Cholesterol; 14 g Carbohydrate; 1 g Fibre; 3 g Protein; 174 mg Sodium

Mango Ribs

Mango gives these tender, tasty ribs a sweet and fruity flavour twist—perfect for a simple, hands-on appetizer at a casual get-together.

Frozen mango pieces, thawed	1 cup	250 mL
Prepared chicken broth	1 cup	250 mL
Mango chutney	1/2 cup	125 mL
Brown sugar, packed	1 tbsp.	15 mL
Sweet-and-sour-cut pork ribs, trimmed of fat and cut into 1-bone portions	3 1/2 lbs.	1.6 kg

Combine first 4 ingredients in 4 to 5 quart (4 to 5 L) slow cooker.

Arrange ribs on greased baking sheet with sides. Sprinkle with salt and pepper. Broil on top rack in oven for about 7 minutes per side until lightly browned. Drain and discard liquid. Add ribs to slow cooker. Stir. Cook, covered, on Low for 6 to 7 hours or on High for 3 to 3 1/2 hours. Transfer ribs with slotted spoon to medium bowl. Cover to keep warm. Skim and discard fat from cooking liquid. Carefully process in blender until smooth (see Safety Tip). Pour over ribs. Makes about 6 cups (1.5 L).

1/2 cup (125 mL): 567 Calories; 41.3 g Total Fat (17.9 g Mono, 3.7 g Poly, 14.7 g Sat); 160 mg Cholesterol; 8 g Carbohydrate; trace Fibre; 39 g Protein; 399 mg Sodium

Safety Tip: Follow manufacturer's instructions for processing hot liquids.

Paré Pointer

The chicken had poor vision. She was trying to hatch an eggplant.

Cajun-Spiced Nuts

The spicy heat of Cajun seasoning pairs well with the roasted crunch of this flavourful, nutty snack.

Raw cashews	1 1/2 cups	375 mL
Whole natural almonds	1 1/2 cups	375 mL
Pecan halves	1 cup	250 mL
Butter (or hard margarine), melted	1/4 cup	60 mL
Cajun seasoning	2 tbsp.	30 mL

Combine all 5 ingredients and a sprinkle of salt in 3 1/2 to 4 quart (3.5 to 4 L) slow cooker. Cook, covered, on Low for 2 hours. Stir well. Cook, covered, on High for about 1 hour, stirring occasionally, until nuts are browned. Spread on ungreased baking sheet to cool and crisp. Makes about 4 cups (1 L).

1/4 cup (60 mL): 217 Calories; 19.8 g Total Fat (10.9 g Mono, 4.0 g Poly, 4.0 g Sat); 8 mg Cholesterol; 8 g Carbohydrate; 2 g Fibre; 5 g Protein; 262 mg Sodium

Hot Crab Dip

This tomato-topped, cheesy crab dip will be a hit at any gathering. Scoop up tasty mouthfuls with toasted baguette rounds, pita crisps or crackers.

Cream cheese, softened	1 1/2 cups	375 mL
Cans of crabmeat (6 oz., 170 g, each), drained, cartilage removed, flaked	2	2
Grated Asiago (or Parmesan) cheese	1 cup	250 mL
Diced seeded Roma (plum) tomato	1 cup	250 mL
Finely chopped green onion	2 tbsp.	30 mL

Combine first 3 ingredients in 3 1/2 to 4 quart (3.5 to 4 L) slow cooker. Cook, covered, on Low for about 2 hours or on High for about 1 hour, stirring twice, until heated through. Transfer to serving dish.

Combine tomato, onion and a sprinkle of salt in small bowl. Spoon over crab mixture. Makes about 3 1/2 cups (875 mL).

1/4 cup (60 mL): 144 Calories; 7.5 g Total Fat (0.1 g Mono, 0.1 g Poly, 7.5 g Sat); 54 mg Cholesterol; 2 g Carbohydrate; trace Fibre; 9 g Protein; 286 mg Sodium

Pictured on page 17.

Mexi Meatballs

Serve these tasty appetizer meatballs with toothpicks and enjoy! Choose your own level of heat by using mild, medium or hot salsa. Meatballs should be thawed overnight in the refrigerator.

Box of frozen cooked meatballs, thawed	2 lbs.	900 g
Salsa	2 cups	500 mL
Sour cream	1/2 cup	125 mL
Lime juice	2 tbsp.	30 mL
Chopped fresh cilantro (or parsley)	1 tbsp.	15 mL

Combine meatballs and salsa in 3 1/2 to 4 quart (3.5 to 4 L) slow cooker. Cook, covered, on Low for 3 to 4 hours or on High for 1 1/2 to 2 hours.

Combine remaining 3 ingredients in small bowl. Add to meatball mixture. Stir. Serves 12.

1 serving: 274 Calories; 19.4 g Total Fat (0 g Mono, 0 g Poly, 8.3 g Sat); 42 mg Cholesterol; 10 g Carbohydrate; 2 g Fibre; 4 g Protein; 824 mg Sodium

Smokin' Smokies

A triple hit of smoky flavour with smoked sausages, chipotle peppers and smoked paprika—and some chili spice too! Serve from the slow cooker on lowest setting with a generous supply of toothpicks.

Cocktail-sized smokies (or regular smokies, cut diagonally into 1/2 inch, 12 mm, slices)	2 lbs.	900 g
Chili sauce	1 3/4 cups	425 mL
Brown sugar, packed	1 tbsp.	15 mL
Finely chopped chipotle peppers in adobo sauce (see Tip, page 141)	1 tbsp.	15 mL
Smoked sweet paprika	2 tsp.	10 mL

Combine all 5 ingredients in 3 1/2 to 4 quart (3.5 to 4 L) slow cooker. Cook, covered, on Low for 6 to 7 hours or on High for 3 to 3 1/2 hours. Makes about 5 cups (1.25 L).

1/3 cup (75 mL): 224 Calories; 16.7 g Total Fat (0 g Mono, 0 g Poly, 5.8 g Sat); 36 mg Cholesterol; 11 g Carbohydrate; trace Fibre; 7 g Protein; 1396 mg Sodium

Pictured on page 71.

Red-Peppered Chorizo

This creamy sausage and cheese mixture tastes great on crisp crackers or crostini slices for a hearty snack or appetizer. Goat cheese and zesty orange pair well with the spicy sausage.

Chorizo (or hot Italian) sausage, casing removed	1 1/2 lbs.	680 g
Jar of roasted red peppers, drained, chopped	12 oz.	340 mL
Balsamic vinaigrette dressing	2 tbsp.	30 mL
Frozen concentrated orange juice, thawed	2 tbsp.	30 mL
Goat (chèvre) cheese	1/3 cup	75 mL

Scramble-fry sausage in large frying pan on medium-high for about 12 minutes until no longer pink. Drain. Transfer to 3 1/2 to 4 quart (3.5 to 4 L) slow cooker.

Add next 3 ingredients. Stir. Cook, covered, on Low for 3 to 4 hours or on High for 1 1/2 to 2 hours.

Add cheese. Stir until melted. Makes about 2 1/2 cups (625 mL).

1/4 cup (60 mL): 304 Calories; 20.2 g Total Fat (8.5 g Mono, 2.3 g Poly, 7.6 g Sat); 42 mg Cholesterol; 11 g Carbohydrate; trace Fibre; 16 g Protein; 1191 mg Sodium

Pictured on page 71.

Vanilla Chai Temptation

This smooth and creamy treat is perfect with a plate of sweets at a book club meeting, or to unwind with after a family day of winter activities. Turn your slow cooker to the Low or Warm setting to maintain serving temperature.

Chai tea bags	10	10
Vanilla bean	1	1
Whole green cardamom, bruised (see Tip, below)	12	12
Canned evaporated milk	3 cups	750 mL
Honey	1/4 cup	60 mL

Pour 6 cups (1.5 L) of water into 3 1/2 to 4 quart (3.5 to 4 L) slow cooker. Put first 3 ingredients onto 12 inch (25 cm) square piece of cheesecloth. Draw up corners and tie with butcher's string. Submerge in water. Cook, covered, on Low for 4 to 5 hours or on High for 2 to 2 1/2 hours. Remove and discard cheesecloth bag.

Add evaporated milk and honey. Stir. Cook, covered, on High for 30 minutes until heated through. Makes about 9 cups (2.25 L).

1 cup (250 mL): 137 Calories; 5.3 g Total Fat (1.1 g Mono, 0.2 g Poly, 4.0 g Sat); 27 mg Cholesterol; 16 g Carbohydrate; 0 g Fibre; 5 g Protein; 80 mg Sodium

 To bruise cardamom, pound pods with mallet or press with flat side of wide knife to "bruise," or crack them open slightly.

Pomegranate Cheer

This dark, jewel-toned beverage is ideal for entertaining during the holidays—try adding lemon vodka, vanilla liqueur or port for a grown-up twist.

Apple juice	4 cups	1 L
Pomegranate juice	4 cups	1 L
Orange juice	1 cup	250 mL
Brown sugar, packed	1/3 cup	75 mL
Slices of ginger root	3	3
(about 1/4 inch, 6 mm, thick)		

Combine all 5 ingredients in 3 1/2 to 4 quart (3.5 to 4 L) slow cooker. Cook, covered, on Low for 4 to 6 hours or on High for 2 to 3 hours. Remove and discard ginger with slotted spoon. Makes about 9 1/3 cups (2.4 L).

1 cup (250 mL): 149 Calories; 0.1 g Total Fat (trace Mono, trace Poly, trace Sat); 0 mg Cholesterol; 38 g Carbohydrate; trace Fibre; 1 g Protein; 16 mg Sodium

Hot Mulled Cider

The classic flavours of spiced hot cider will warm everyone up on a blustery snow day.

Sweet apple cider	8 cups	2 L
Brown sugar, packed	1/4 cup	60 mL
Large orange, cut into 1/4 inch	1	1
(6 mm) slices		
Cinnamon sticks (4 inches, 10 cm, each)	2	2
Whole allspice	1 tsp.	5 mL

Combine cider and brown sugar in 3 1/2 to 4 quart (3.5 to 4 L) slow cooker.

Put remaining 3 ingredients onto 12 inch (30 cm) square piece of cheesecloth. Draw up corners and tie with butcher's string. Submerge in cider mixture. Cook, covered, on Low for 5 to 6 hours or on High for 2 1/2 to 3 hours. Remove and discard cheesecloth bag. Makes about 6 1/2 cups (1.6 L).

1 cup (250 mL): 180 Calories; 0 g Total Fat (0 g Mono, 0 g Poly, 0 g Sat); 0 mg Cholesterol; 45 g Carbohydrate; 0 g Fibre; 0 g Protein; 34 mg Sodium

Sweet Spiced Coffee

This sweet coffee was inspired by Vietnamese coffee, which is strong French roasted coffee with sweetened condensed milk. The added dimension of aromatic spices gives this an exotic flair. It's delicious served over ice, too!

Whole green cardamom, bruised (see Tip, page 25)	5	5
Cinnamon sticks (4 inches, 10 cm, each)	2	2
Star anise	1	1
Instant coffee granules	1 cup	250 mL
Cans of sweetened condensed milk (11 oz., 300 mL, each)	2	2

Combine first 3 ingredients and 8 cups (2 L) water in 3 1/2 to 4 quart (3.5 to 4 L) slow cooker. Cook, covered, on Low for 3 to 4 hours or on High for 1 1/2 to 2 hours. Remove and discard spices with slotted spoon.

Add coffee granules. Stir until dissolved. Add condensed milk. Stir until smooth. Makes about 11 cups (2.75 L).

1 cup (250 mL): 203 Calories; 4.5 g Total Fat (0 g Mono, trace Poly, 3.0 g Sat); 15 mg Cholesterol; 34 g Carbohydrate; 0 g Fibre; 5 g Protein; 69 mg Sodium

Warm and Fuzzy Navel

Serve this in a punchbowl for a cozy winter brunch, or hand it out as a welcoming cocktail for a holiday party.

Apricot fruit juice blend	6 cups	1.5 L
Orange juice	6 cups	1.5 L
Grenadine syrup (optional)	1 tbsp.	15 mL
Orange liqueur	3/4 cup	175 mL
Peach schnapps	3/4 cup	175 mL

Combine first 3 ingredients in 3 1/2 to 4 quart (3.5 to 4 L) slow cooker. Cook, covered, on Low for 2 to 4 hours or on High for 1 to 2 hours.

Add liqueur and schnapps. Stir. Makes about 13 1/2 cups (3.4 L).

1 cup (250 mL): 183 Calories; 0.3 g Total Fat (0.1 g Mono, 0.1 g Poly, trace Sat); 0 mg Cholesterol; 35 g Carbohydrate; trace Fibre; 1 g Protein; 9 mg Sodium

Pictured on page 18.

Coconut Rum Mocha

This is a delightful chocolate coffee with a hint of coconut and rum—a just-for-grown-ups treat after the sleigh-ride.

Chocolate milk	6 cups	1.5 L
Strong prepared coffee	6 cups	1.5 L
Coconut rum	1 1/4 cups	300 mL
Whipped cream (or whipped topping)	1 1/2 cups	375 mL
Medium sweetened coconut, toasted (see Tip, page 146)	2 tbsp.	30 mL

Combine chocolate milk and coffee in 3 1/2 to 4 quart (3.5 to 4 L) slow cooker. Cook, covered, on Low for 4 to 5 hours or on High for 2 to 2 1/2 hours.

Add coconut rum. Stir. Makes about 13 1/4 cups (3.3 L)

Pour into 12 large mugs. Spoon whipped cream over top. Sprinkle with coconut. Serves 12.

1 serving: 266 Calories; 13.8 g Total Fat (3.2 g Mono, 0.4 g Poly, 8.6 g Sat); 53 mg Cholesterol; 18 g Carbohydrate; 1 g Fibre; 5 g Protein; 141 mg Sodium

Variation: Omit coconut rum and sweetened coconut. Substitute same amount of vanilla liqueur and vanilla sugar or cocoa.

Variation: Omit coconut rum and sweetened coconut. Substitute same amount of hazelnut liqueur and sprinkle with flaked hazelnuts or cocoa.

Hazelnut Hot Chocolate

This silky, rich hot chocolate has a hint of hazelnut for a European flair. Liqueur-scented whipped cream transforms it into an adult treat, but the liqueur can be omitted for a kid-friendly winter warmer.

Milk	12 cups	3 L
Chocolate hazelnut spread	2 cups	500 mL
Whipping cream	1 cup	250 mL
Hazelnut liqueur	2 tbsp.	30 mL
Granulated sugar	2 tbsp.	30 mL

(continued on next page)

Combine milk and chocolate hazelnut spread in 4 to 5 quart (4 to 5 L) slow cooker. Cook, covered, on Low for 4 to 5 hours or on High for 2 to 2 1/2 hours until heated through. Stir until smooth. Makes about 14 cups (3.5 L). Pour into 12 large mugs.

Beat remaining 3 ingredients in medium bowl until stiff peaks form. Spoon over milk mixture. Serves 12.

1 serving: 399 Calories; 21.1 g Total Fat (9.3 g Mono, 2.8 g Poly, 8.1 g Sat); 42 mg Cholesterol; 40 g Carbohydrate; 2 g Fibre; 11 g Protein; 153 mg Sodium

Mulled Blackcurrant Sipper

While cinnamon, cloves and allspice are typically used for mulling, aniseed and star anise impart a lovely hint of licorice that pairs well with blackcurrant.

White cranberry juice	10 cups	2.5 L
Concentrated blackcurrant nectar	2 cups	500 mL
Aniseed	1 tbsp.	15 mL
Star anise	2	2
Brown sugar, packed (optional)	1 tbsp.	15 mL

Combine juice and nectar in 4 to 5 quart (4 to 5 L) slow cooker.

Put aniseed and star anise onto 5 inch (12.5 cm) square piece of cheesecloth. Draw up corners and tie with butcher's string. Submerge in cranberry juice mixture. Cook, covered, on Low for 6 to 8 hours or on High for 3 to 4 hours. Remove and discard cheesecloth bag.

Add brown sugar. Stir. Makes about 12 cups (3 L).

1 cup (250 mL): 115 Calories; 0 g Total Fat (0 g Mono, 0 g Poly, 0 g Sat); 0 mg Cholesterol; 27 g Carbohydrate; 0 g Fibre; trace Protein; 15 mg Sodium

Pictured on page 18.

Paré Pointer
Noah kept bees in ark-hives.

Peppermint Hot Chocolate

Pull a candy cane off the tree for this decadent holiday treat.
Creamy chocolate and peppermint make a deliciously sweet pair!

Milk	6 cups	1.5 L
Chocolate-covered peppermint patties, chopped	2 cups	500 mL
Chocolate milk	2 cups	500 mL
Whipped cream (or whipped topping)	1 cup	250 mL
Finely crushed candy cane	2 tbsp.	30 mL

Combine first 3 ingredients in 3 1/2 to 4 quart (3.5 to 4 L) slow cooker. Cook, covered, on Low for 4 to 5 hours or on High for 2 to 2 1/2 hours. Stir. Makes about 8 cups (2 L).

Pour into 8 mugs. Spoon whipped cream over top. Sprinkle with crushed candy cane. Serves 8.

1 serving: 474 Calories; 18.3 g Total Fat (4.2 g Mono, 0.5 g Poly, 11.2 g Sat); 59 mg Cholesterol; 68 g Carbohydrate; 1 g Fibre; 11 g Protein; 197 mg Sodium

Hot Fruit Punch

Treat the kids to a mug of this warming winter beverage after they've finished shoveling that snowed-in sidewalk!

Apple juice	4 cups	1 L
Cranberry cocktail	4 cups	1 L
Pineapple juice	4 cups	1 L
Cinnamon stick (4 inches, 10 cm), broken up	1	1
Whole allspice	1 tsp.	5 mL

Combine first 3 ingredients in 3 1/2 to 4 quart (3.5 to 4 L) slow cooker.

Put cinnamon stick pieces and allspice onto 6 inch (15 cm) square piece of cheesecloth. Draw up corners and tie with butcher's string. Submerge in juice mixture. Cook, covered, on Low for 4 to 6 hours or on High for 2 to 3 hours. Remove and discard cheesecloth bag. Makes about 12 cups (3 L).

1 cup (250 mL): 127 Calories; 0 g Total Fat (0 g Mono, 0 g Poly, 0 g Sat); 0 mg Cholesterol; 32 g Carbohydrate; 0 g Fibre; 0 g Protein; 2 mg Sodium

Pictured on page 18.

Chocolate Peanut Delight

This hot-chocolatey drink is topped with whipped cream and peanuts, for all the chocolate-with-peanut butter lovers out there—kids will love it too!

Chocolate milk powder	1 cup	250 mL
Smooth peanut butter	1/2 cup	125 mL
Milk	8 cups	2 L
Whipped cream (or whipped topping)	1 cup	250 mL
Finely chopped unsalted peanuts	2 tsp.	10 mL

Stir first 3 ingredients in 3 1/2 to 4 quart (3.5 to 4 L) slow cooker until milk powder is dissolved. Cook, covered, on Low for 4 to 5 hours or on High for 2 to 2 1/2 hours until heated through and peanut butter is melted. Whisk until combined. Makes about 9 1/2 cups (2.4 L)

Pour into 8 mugs. Spoon whipped cream over top. Sprinkle with peanuts. Serves 8.

1 serving: 417 Calories; 22.8 g Total Fat (4.4 g Mono, 0.5 g Poly, 10.2 g Sat); 56 mg Cholesterol; 41 g Carbohydrate; 1 g Fibre; 16 g Protein; 289 mg Sodium

Pictured on page 144.

Ginger Citrus Tonic

This mixture of tea, calming ginger and antibacterial, throat-soothing honey works wonders on a cold. Rooibos tea is antioxidant-rich and caffeine-free, but mint tea also works well. Remove the solids, and keep a batch hot on Low for up to 12 hours.

Lemon slices (1/4 inch, 6 mm, thick)	1 cup	250 mL
Orange slices (1/4 inch, 6 mm, thick)	1 cup	250 mL
Liquid honey	1/3 cup	75 mL
Sliced ginger root (1/4 inch, 6 mm, thick)	1/4 cup	60 mL
Vanilla rooibos teabags	4	4

Combine all 5 ingredients in 3 1/2 to 4 quart (3.5 to 4 L) slow cooker. Add 8 cups (2 L) of water. Cook, covered, on Low for 5 to 6 hours or on High for 2 1/2 to 3 hours. Remove and discard solids with slotted spoon. Makes about 8 cups (2 L).

1 cup (250 mL): 45 Calories; 0 g Total Fat (0 g Mono, 0 g Poly, 0 g Sat); 0 mg Cholesterol; 11 g Carbohydrate; 0 g Fibre; 0 g Protein; 0 mg Sodium

Beverages

Allspice Mulled Wine

The flavours of cinnamon and orange stand out in this spicy beverage. Sipping some around the fireplace will warm you right down to your toes.

Dry (or alcohol-free) red wine	6 cups	1.5 L
Can of frozen concentrated cranberry cocktail	9 1/2 oz.	275 mL
Medium orange, sliced	1	1
Cinnamon sticks (4 inches, 10 cm, each)	2	2
Whole allspice	6	6

Combine wine, cranberry cocktail and 2 cups (500 mL) water in 3 1/2 to 4 quart (3.5 to 4 L) slow cooker.

Put remaining 3 ingredients onto 12 inch (30 cm) square piece of cheesecloth. Draw up corners and tie with butcher's string. Submerge in wine mixture. Cook, covered, on Low for 5 to 6 hours or on High for 2 1/2 to 3 hours. Remove and discard cheesecloth bag. Makes about 9 1/3 cups (2.4 L).

1 cup (250 mL): 185 Calories; 0 g Total Fat (0 g Mono, 0 g Poly, 0 g Sat); 0 mg Cholesterol; 18 g Carbohydrate; trace Fibre; trace Protein; 7 mg Sodium

Paré Pointer
Mother ghost to little ghost: "Don't spook until you're spooken to."

Ruby Beet Soup

The flavours of pears and beets complement each other in this velvety,
beautifully coloured soup. Add a sour cream garnish, or try serving it chilled
for a refreshing variation.

Chopped onion	3/4 cup	175 mL
Chopped fresh peeled beet (see Note)	6 cups	1.5 L
Prepared vegetable broth	4 cups	1 L
Can of pear halves, drained and juice reserved	28 oz.	796 mL
Red wine vinegar	2 tbsp.	30 mL

Heat medium greased frying pan on medium. Add onion. Cook for about 5 minutes, stirring often, until softened. Transfer to 3 1/2 to 4 quart (3.5 to 4 L) slow cooker.

Add next 3 ingredients. Cook, covered, on Low for 8 to 9 hours or High for 4 to 4 1/2 hours until beet is tender.

Add vinegar and reserved pear juice. Stir. Carefully process with hand blender or in blender in batches until smooth (see Safety Tip). Makes about 9 1/2 cups (2.4 L).

1 cup (250 mL): 93 Calories; 0.9 g Total Fat (0.3 g Mono, 0.2 g Poly, 0.1 g Sat); 0 mg Cholesterol; 21 g Carbohydrate; 3 g Fibre; 2 g Protein; 383 mg Sodium

Pictured on page 35.

Note: Don't get caught red handed! Wear rubber gloves when handling beets.

Safety Tip: Follow manufacturer's instructions for processing hot liquids.

Lamb and Barley Soup

Also known as Scottish broth, this warming soup is a centuries-old favourite.

Lamb shanks, trimmed of fat, cut into 1/2 inch (12 mm) pieces, bones reserved (see Note 1)	1 lb.	454 g
Diced carrot (1/4 inch, 6mm, pieces)	1 cup	250 mL
Diced yellow turnip (rutabaga)	1 cup	250 mL
Pot barley	1/2 cup	125 mL
Envelope of onion soup mix	1 1/2 oz.	42 g

Heat greased large frying pan on medium-high. Add lamb. Cook for about 8 minutes, stirring occasionally, until browned. Transfer to 4 to 5 quart (4 to 5 L) slow cooker. Add 1 1/2 cups (375 mL) water to same frying pan. Heat and stir, scraping any brown bits from bottom of pan, until boiling. Pour over lamb.

Add next 4 ingredients, reserved bones, 5 cups (1.25 L) water and a sprinkle of salt and pepper. Stir. Cook, covered, on Low for 8 to 10 hours or on High for 4 to 5 hours. Remove and discard bones. Makes about 7 1/2 cups (1.9 L).

1 cup (250 mL): 131 Calories; 3.9 g Total Fat (1.7 g Mono, 0.4 g Poly, 1.2 g Sat); 21 mg Cholesterol; 16 g Carbohydrate; 3 g Fibre; 8 g Protein; 631 mg Sodium

Pictured on page 36.

Note 1: Lamb shanks are commonly found in frozen bulk packages. If using frozen shanks, remember to thaw them before using. If shank is not available, lamb shoulder or even beef stew meat can be substituted.

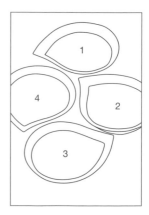

Smoky Salmon Potato Soup

This smooth, smoky-tasting soup was inspired by Cullen Skink, a soup from the Scottish village of Cullen. It is traditionally made with smoked haddock, and has kept generations of people warm on cold, rainy nights. Sprinkle with chopped fresh parsley to serve.

Finely chopped onion	1 1/2 cups	375 mL
Diced, peeled baking potato	4 cups	1 L
Prepared vegetable broth	3 cups	750 mL
Milk	2 cups	500 mL
Thinly sliced smoked salmon, chopped	4 oz.	113 g

Heat large greased frying pan on medium. Add onion. Cook for about 8 minutes, stirring often, until softened. Transfer to 3 1/2 to 4 quart (3.5 to 4 L) slow cooker.

Add potato and broth. Cook, covered, on Low for 5 to 6 hours or on High for 2 1/2 to 3 hours until potato is tender.

Carefully process with hand blender or in blender in batches until smooth (see Safety Tip). Add milk and smoked salmon. Cook, covered, on High for about 15 minutes until heated through. Sprinkle generously with salt and pepper. Stir. Makes about 8 cups (2 L).

1 cup (250 mL): 171 Calories; 2.2 g Total Fat (0.9 g Mono, 0.4 g Poly, 0.6 g Sat); 7 mg Cholesterol; 31 g Carbohydrate; 3 g Fibre; 7 g Protein; 735 mg Sodium

Safety Tip: Follow manufacturer's instructions for processing hot liquids.

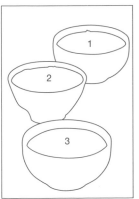

1. Lamb and Barley Soup, page 34
2. Smoked Pork and Bean Soup, page 38
3. Split Pea Soup, page 42

Lobster Chowder

This thick, creamy chowder makes an elegant starter for a dinner party when you want something extra-special for your guests. Using the slow cooker will also leave the stove free for all your other dishes.

Chopped onion	2 cups	500 mL
Diced peeled baking potato	4 cups	1 L
Prepared vegetable broth	4 cups	1 L
Can of frozen lobster meat (with liquid), thawed, larger pieces cut up	11 1/3 oz.	320 g
Evaporated milk (or half-and-half cream)	1 1/2 cups	375 mL

Heat large greased frying pan on medium. Add onion and a generous sprinkle of salt and pepper. Cook for about 10 minutes, stirring often, until softened. Transfer to 4 to 5 quart (4 to 5 L) slow cooker.

Add next 3 ingredients to slow cooker. Stir. Cook, covered, on Low for 6 to 7 hours or on High for 3 to 3 1/2 hours. Break up mixture with potato masher.

Add evaporated milk. Stir. Makes about 9 cups (2.25 L).

1 cup (250 mL): 213 Calories; 4.1 g Total Fat (1.0 g Mono, 0.5 g Poly, 2.2 g Sat); 38 mg Cholesterol; 31 g Carbohydrate; 3 g Fibre; 13 g Protein; 681 mg Sodium

Smoked Pork and Bean Soup

Enjoy this hearty soup with a slice of multi-grain bread for dipping. Buy a packaged bean mix or create your own custom mixture. Make sure about a third of it is split peas and/or red lentils because these legumes break up during cooking, giving the soup a great texture.

Dried mixed beans and lentils	1 1/2 cups	375 mL
Smoked pork hock (or meaty ham bone)	1 1/2 lbs.	680 g
Chopped onion	1 cup	250 mL
Can of diced tomatoes (with juice)	14 oz.	398 mL
Envelope of vegetable soup mix	1 1/4 oz.	40 g

(continued on next page)

Measure beans and lentils into medium bowl. Add water until 2 inches (5 cm) above beans. Let stand overnight (see Tip, page 15). Drain. Rinse beans. Drain. Transfer to 5 to 7 quart (5 to 7 L) slow cooker.

Add pork hock, onion and 9 cups (2.25 L) water. Cook, covered, on High for 4 to 5 hours until beans are tender. Remove pork hock. Let stand until cool enough to handle. Remove and discard skin, bones and fat. Chop meat. Return to slow cooker.

Add tomatoes, soup mix and a sprinkle of salt and pepper. Stir. Cook, covered, on High for about 45 minutes until vegetables are tender. Makes about 13 1/2 cups (3.4 L).

1 cup (250 mL): 219 Calories; 12.1 g Total Fat (5.2 g Mono, 1.2 g Poly, 4.4 g Sat); 55 mg Cholesterol; 10 g Carbohydrate; 3 g Fibre; 17 g Protein; 304 mg Sodium

Pictured on page 36.

Sweet Onion Soup

An easy take on onion soup—and no need to caramelize the onions on the stove! For a real treat, serve this delicious soup with slices of toast topped with melted smoked cheddar or havarti.

Thinly sliced sweet onion (see Note 1)	6 cups	1.5 L
Olive (or cooking) oil	3 tbsp.	50 mL
Prepared beef broth (see Note 2)	6 cups	1.5 L
Dark beer	1 1/2 cups	375 mL
Sprig of fresh thyme	1	1
(or 1/2 tsp., 2 mL, dried)		

Combine onion and olive oil in 3 1/2 to 4 quart (3.5 to 4 L) slow cooker. Cook, covered, on High for about 6 hours, stirring once at halftime, until onion is caramelized.

Add next 3 ingredients and a sprinkle of salt and pepper. Cook, covered, on High for about 45 minutes until heated through. Remove and discard thyme sprig. Makes about 8 3/4 cups (2.2 L).

1 cup (250 mL): 122 Calories; 5.4 g Total Fat (3.6 g Mono, 0.7 g Poly, 0.9 g Sat); 0 mg Cholesterol; 15 g Carbohydrate; 1 g Fibre; 2 g Protein; 1017 mg Sodium

Note 1: If you prefer not to have long strands of onion, cut onions in half before slicing for shorter strands.

Note 2: When adding liquid to a hot slow cooker, make sure the liquid is at least room temperature, as cold liquids could cause the liner to crack.

Soups

Curried Pumpkin Soup

This thick, creamy soup has apple cider sweetness and a touch of curry heat.
With a dollop of sour cream, it's an attractive starter for a holiday meal.

Finely chopped onion	1 1/2 cups	375 mL
Cans of pure pumpkin (no spices), 14 oz. (398 mL) each	2	2
Prepared chicken broth	2 cups	500 mL
Sweet apple cider	2 cups	500 mL
Mild curry paste	2 tsp.	10 mL

Heat large greased frying pan on medium. Add onion. Cook for about 8 minutes, stirring often, until softened. Transfer to 3 1/2 to 4 quart (3.5 to 4 L) slow cooker.

Add remaining 4 ingredients. Stir. Cook, covered, on Low for 5 to 6 hours or on High for 2 1/2 to 3 hours. Sprinkle with salt and pepper. Carefully process with hand blender or in blender in batches until smooth (see Safety Tip). Makes about 8 cups (2 L).

1 cup (250 mL): 90 Calories; 1.4 g Total Fat (0.5 g Mono, 0.3 g Poly, 0.3 g Sat); 0 mg Cholesterol; 19 g Carbohydrate; 3 g Fibre; 2 g Protein; 500 mg Sodium

Safety Tip: Follow manufacturer's instructions for processing liquids.

Kielbasa Potato Soup

This wholesome soup is thick with cooked-down potato and makes a meal
when served with crusty bread. The longer it stands, the more
the flavours blend.

Chopped peeled potato	6 cups	1.5 L
Prepared vegetable broth	4 cups	1 L
Kielbasa (or other spiced cooked lean sausage), thinly sliced	3/4 lb.	340 g
Garlic and herb no-salt seasoning	1/2 tsp.	2 mL
Frozen cut green beans, thawed	1 1/2 cups	375 mL

(continued on next page)

Combine first 4 ingredients and 2 cups (500 mL) water in 5 to 7 quart (5 to 7 L) slow cooker. Sprinkle generously with salt and pepper. Cook, covered, on Low for 10 to 11 hours or on High for 5 to 5 1/2 hours.

Add green beans. Stir. Cook, covered, on High for about 30 minutes until tender. Break up with potato masher. Makes about 11 cups (2.75 L).

1 cup (250 mL): 161 Calories; 1.1 g Total Fat (0 g Mono, 0.1 g Poly, 0.3 g Sat); 11 mg Cholesterol; 31 g Carbohydrate; 1 g Fibre; 7 g Protein; 853 mg Sodium

---

Chipotle Corn Chowder

The sweet aroma of this soup will bring a southwestern feel to your kitchen! Enjoy the richness of creamed corn and the flavour of smoky bacon and chipotle peppers.

Chopped onion	1 cup	250 mL
Bacon slices, diced	6	6
Cans of cream-style corn (14 oz., 398 mL, each)	3	3
Can of red kidney beans, rinsed and drained	14 oz.	398 mL
Finely chopped chipotle peppers in adobo sauce (see Tip, below)	1 tbsp.	15 mL

Heat medium frying pan on medium-high. Add onion and bacon. Cook for about 5 minutes, stirring often, until onion is softened. Transfer to 3 1/2 to 4 quart (3.5 to 4 L) slow cooker.

Add remaining 3 ingredients and 2 1/2 cups (625 mL) water. Stir. Cook, covered, on Low for 6 to 7 hours or on High for 3 to 3 1/2 hours. Makes about 8 1/2 cups (2.1 L).

1 cup (250 mL): 198 Calories; 2.7 g Total Fat (0.8 g Mono, 0.2 g Poly, 0.6 g Sat); 5 mg Cholesterol; 36 g Carbohydrate; 6 g Fibre; 7 g Protein; 586 mg Sodium

 tip Chipotle chili peppers are smoked jalapeño peppers. Be sure to wash your hands after handling. To store leftover chipotle chili peppers, divide into recipe-friendly portions and freeze, with sauce, in airtight containers for up to one year.

Split Pea Soup

This simple, classic soup has lots of smoky sausage flavour and a hint of garlic. It can be cooked on Low, but it will take twelve hours or more for the peas to soften.

Chopped carrots	2 cups	500 mL
Yellow split peas, rinsed and drained	2 cups	500 mL
Diced kielbasa (or other spiced cooked lean sausage)	1 1/2 cups	375 mL
Chopped celery (with leaves)	3/4 cup	175 mL
Chopped onion	3/4 cup	175 mL

Combine all 5 ingredients in 3 1/2 to 4 quart (3.5 to 4 L) slow cooker. Add 8 cups (2 L) water. Stir. Cook, covered, on High for 6 to 7 hours until peas are tender. Sprinkle generously with salt and pepper. Stir. Makes about 9 cups (2.25 L).

1 cup (250 mL): 223 Calories; 1.1 g Total Fat (trace Mono, 0.1 g Poly, 0.4 g Sat); 13 mg Cholesterol; 37 g Carbohydrate; 1 g Fibre; 17 g Protein; 480 mg Sodium

Pictured on page 36.

Tortilla Soup

This creamy, cheesy soup has a nacho twist with crunchy tortilla chips in every bowl—a perfect starter for a casual or Mexican-themed party. Adjust the heat by choosing mild, medium or hot salsa.

Prepared chicken broth	4 cups	1 L
Chunky salsa	1 1/2 cups	375 mL
Can of condensed Cheddar cheese soup	10 oz.	284 mL
Sour cream	2/3 cup	150 mL
Tortilla chips, broken up	1 cup	250 mL

Combine first 3 ingredients in 3 1/2 to 4 quart (3.5 to 4 L) slow cooker. Cook, covered, on Low for 4 to 6 hours or on High for 2 to 3 hours.

Add sour cream. Stir until smooth.

Put tortilla chips into 4 soup bowls. Ladle soup over chips. Serves 4.

1 serving: 260 Calories; 13.9 g Total Fat (1.4 g Mono, 1.5 g Poly, 6.8 g Sat); 32 mg Cholesterol; 27 g Carbohydrate; 1 g Fibre; 5 g Protein; 2834 mg Sodium

Soups

Orange Sweet Potato Soup

Serve this thick, creamy and vibrant soup either warm or chilled. Cilantro lovers might enjoy a sprinkle of this fresh herb in their bowls.

Fresh peeled orange-fleshed sweet potatoes, chopped	3 lbs.	1.4 kg
Prepared vegetable broth	4 cups	1 L
Chopped onion	1 cup	250 mL
Large oranges	2	2
Plain yogurt	1 cup	250 mL

Combine sweet potato and broth in 3 1/2 to 4 quart (3.5 to 4 L) slow cooker.

Heat medium greased frying pan on medium. Add onion. Cook for about 5 minutes, stirring often, until softened. Add to slow cooker. Cook, covered, on Low for 6 to 7 hours or on High for 3 to 3 1/2 hours.

Grate 1/2 tsp. (2 mL) orange zest into small bowl. Squeeze orange juice into same bowl. Add to slow cooker. Carefully process with hand blender or in blender in batches until almost smooth (see Safety Tip).

Add yogurt. Stir. Makes about 10 cups (2.5 L).

1 cup (250 mL): 158 Calories; 1.1 g Total Fat (0.3 g Mono, 0.2 g Poly, 0.3 g Sat); 2 mg Cholesterol; 33 g Carbohydrate; 5 g Fibre; 4 g Protein; 276 mg Sodium

Pictured on page 35.

Safety Tip: Follow manufacturer's instructions for processing hot liquids.

Paré Pointer

That man invented something that allows people to see through walls—he calls it a window.

Apricot Red Lentil Soup

This simple vegetarian soup, Armenian in origin, is a lovely balance of sweet and peppery flavours. It's low-fat, high-fibre and thick, creamy and satisfying!

Chopped onion	2 cups	500 mL
Prepared vegetable broth	4 cups	1 L
Chopped carrot	2 cups	500 mL
Dried red split lentils	2 cups	500 mL
Chopped dried apricot	1 1/2 cups	375 mL

Heat large greased frying pan on medium. Add onion and a generous sprinkle of salt. Cook for about 15 minutes, stirring often, until onion is browned. Transfer to 5 to 7 quart (5 to 7 L) slow cooker.

Add remaining 4 ingredients and 5 cups (1.25 L) water. Stir. Cook, covered, on Low for 10 to 12 hours or on High for 5 to 6 hours. Carefully process with hand blender or in blender in batches until smooth (see Safety Tip). Makes about 11 cups (2.75 L).

1 cup (250 mL): 206 Calories; 1.4 g Total Fat (0.3 g Mono, 0.2 g Poly, trace Sat); 0 mg Cholesterol; 39 g Carbohydrate; 8 g Fibre; 11 g Protein; 306 mg Sodium

Safety Tip: Follow manufacturer's instructions for processing hot liquids.

Butternut Cream Soup

The sweetness and rich texture of squash and pear blend perfectly with sour cream in this creamy, beautifully golden soup.

Chopped onion	1 1/2 cups	375 mL
Chopped butternut squash	8 cups	2 L
Can of pear halves in juice (with juice)	28 oz.	796 mL
Sour cream	1 cup	250 mL
Chopped fresh chives, for garnish		

Heat large greased frying pan on medium. Add onion. Cook, stirring often, for about 8 minutes until softened. Transfer to 4 to 5 quart (4 to 5 L) slow cooker.

(continued on next page)

Add squash, pears with juice, a generous sprinkle of salt and 2 1/2 cups (625 mL) water. Cook, covered, on Low for 8 to 10 hours or on High for 4 to 5 hours. Carefully process with hand blender or in blender in batches until smooth (see Safety Tip).

Add sour cream. Whisk until smooth. Garnish with chives. Makes about 12 cups (3 L).

1 cup (250 mL): 157 Calories; 3.9 g Total Fat (0.3 g Mono, 0.2 g Poly, 2.4 g Sat); 13 mg Cholesterol; 30 g Carbohydrate; 5 g Fibre; 3 g Protein; 113 mg Sodium

Pictured on page 35.

Safety Tip: Follow manufacturer's instructions for processing hot liquids.

Sausage Kale Soup

This hearty and flavourful soup would serve you well on a chilly winter's evening. For added aroma, look for Italian sausage with fennel seeds for a delicious, licorice-like flavour.

Hot (or mild) Italian sausage, casing removed	3/4 lb.	340 g
Chopped kale leaves, lightly packed (see Tip, page 117)	4 cups	1 L
Can of diced tomatoes (with juice)	28 oz.	796 mL
Can of black-eyed peas (or navy beans), with liquid	19 oz.	540 mL
Basil pesto	1/4 cup	60 mL

Scramble-fry sausage meat in large frying pan on medium for about 10 minutes until no longer pink. Drain. Transfer to 4 to 5 quart (4 to 5 L) slow cooker.

Add next 3 ingredients and 4 cups (1 L) water. Stir. Cook, covered, on Low for 9 to 10 hours or on High for 4 1/2 to 5 hours. Break up mixture with potato masher.

Add pesto. Stir. Makes about 9 3/4 cups (2.4 L).

1 cup (250 mL): 212 Calories; 12.9 g Total Fat (4.2 g Mono, 1.2 g Poly, 3.9 g Sat); 21 mg Cholesterol; 15 g Carbohydrate; 3 g Fibre; 12 g Protein; 958 mg Sodium

Variation: Instead of using sausage with fennel in it, you could also add 2 tsp. (10 mL) whole fennel seeds to the sausage while it's browning.

Meaty Chicken Soup

This is a simple, feel-good soup for when you're under the weather. The broth is very tasty and can be used in other dishes—it also freezes well. Egg noodles or cooked rice may be added for an even heartier soup.

Chicken legs, back attached (11 – 12 oz., 310 – 340 g, each), skin removed	4	4
Chopped onions	2 1/2 cups	625 mL
Chopped celery (with leaves)	1 cup	250 mL
Sprig of fresh rosemary	1	1
Chopped carrot	1 1/2 cups	375 mL

Put chicken into 5 to 7 quart (5 to 7 L) slow cooker. Add next 3 ingredients, 8 cups (2 L) water and a generous sprinkle of salt and pepper. Cook, covered, on Low for 6 hours or on High for 3 hours.

Add carrot. Cook, covered, on High for about 2 hours until chicken and carrot are tender. Remove and discard rosemary. Transfer chicken and bones with slotted spoon to cutting board. Let stand until cool enough to handle. Remove chicken from bones. Discard bones. Coarsely chop chicken. Skim and discard fat from broth. Return chicken to broth. Sprinkle generously with salt and pepper. Stir. Makes about 13 cups (3.25 L).

1 cup (250 mL): 124 Calories; 4.7 g Total Fat (1.7 g Mono, 1.1 g Poly, 1.3 g Sat); 49 mg Cholesterol; 5 g Carbohydrate; 1 g Fibre; 15 g Protein; 245 mg Sodium

---

Paré Pointer
A blister is your heel getting back at you for stepping on it.

Minestrone

This lovely Italian soup doesn't get any easier than when it's made in the slow cooker—serve it with crusty bread and a salad for a light meal.

Prepared vegetable broth	3 cups	750 mL
Frozen mixed vegetables, thawed	2 cups	500 mL
Vegetable cocktail juice	2 cups	500 mL
Italian seasoning	2 tsp.	10 mL
Rotini pasta	1 1/2 cups	375 mL

Combine first 4 ingredients, 1 cup (250 mL) water and a generous sprinkle of pepper in 3 1/2 to 4 quart (3.5 to 4 L) slow cooker. Cook, covered, on Low for 4 to 5 hours or on High for 2 to 2 1/2 hours.

Add pasta. Stir. Cook, covered, on High for 20 to 30 minutes until pasta is tender but firm. Makes about 6 cups (1.5 L).

1 cup (250 mL): 123 Calories; 2.4 g Total Fat (trace Mono, trace Poly, 0.8 g Sat); 3 mg Cholesterol; 22 g Carbohydrate; 2 g Fibre; 4 g Protein; 517 mg Sodium

Chili Shrimp Vegetable Soup

With its cheery, colourful vegetables and tender shrimp, this flavourful, chili-spiced soup would make a great lunch on a cold day.

Frozen Oriental mixed vegetables, thawed larger pieces halved	4 cups	1 L
Prepared vegetable broth	4 cups	1 L
Dried crushed chilies	1/2 tsp.	2 mL
Uncooked medium shrimp (peeled and deveined)	1/2 lb.	225 g
Lime juice	2 tbsp.	30 mL

Combine first 3 ingredients and a generous sprinkle of salt and pepper in 3 1/2 to 4 quart (3.5 to 4 L) slow cooker. Cook, covered, on Low for 2 to 3 hours or on High for 1 to 1 1/2 hours until vegetables are tender-crisp.

Add shrimp. Stir. Cook, covered, on High for about 15 minutes until shrimp turn pink. Add lime juice. Stir. Makes about 6 cups (1.5 L).

1 cup (250 mL): 88 Calories; 1.0 g Total Fat (0.1 g Mono, 0.3 g Poly, 0.1 g Sat); 57 mg Cholesterol; 9 g Carbohydrate; 3 g Fibre; 9 g Protein; 587 mg Sodium

Taco Beef Soup

Serve this hearty meal soup with tortilla chips, a swirl of sour cream and a sprinkle of green onions—and dinner is made!

Stewing beef, trimmed of fat, cut into 1/2 inch (12 mm) pieces	1 lb.	454 g
Chopped onion	1 cup	250 mL
Diced peeled baking potato	3 cups	750 mL
Envelope of taco seasoning mix	1 1/4 oz.	35 g
Frozen mixed vegetables, thawed	1 1/2 cups	375 mL

Heat large greased frying pan on medium-high. Add beef. Cook for about 5 minutes, stirring occasionally, until browned. Transfer to 3 1/2 to 4 quart (3.5 to 4 L) slow cooker.

Add onion to same greased frying pan on medium. Cook for about 5 minutes, stirring often, until softened. Add to slow cooker.

Add potato, seasoning mix and 4 cups (1 L) water. Stir. Cook, covered, on Low for 7 to 8 hours or on High for 3 1/2 to 4 hours. Mash mixture several times with potato masher to break up potato.

Add mixed vegetables. Stir. Cook, covered, on High for about 30 minutes until vegetables are tender. Makes about 8 cups (2 L).

1 cup (250 mL): 227 Calories; 9.4 g Total Fat (3.8 g Mono, 0.6 g Poly, 3.4 g Sat); 37 mg Cholesterol; 23 g Carbohydrate; 2 g Fibre; 12 g Protein; 532 mg Sodium

Mushroom Dill Soup

A light and refreshing combination. Earthy mushrooms blend with the tanginess of dill in a wine-accented broth.

Chopped assorted fresh mushrooms (see Note)	6 cups	1.5 L
Dry (or alcohol-free) white wine	1 cup	250 mL
Prepared vegetable broth	4 cups	1 L
Grated peeled potato	1 1/2 cups	375 mL
Dried dillweed	2 tsp.	10 mL

(continued on next page)

Heat large greased frying pan or Dutch oven on medium-high. Add mushrooms. Cook for about 10 minutes, stirring occasionally, until mushrooms start to brown.

Add wine and a generous sprinkle of salt and pepper. Heat and stir for 2 minutes. Transfer to 3 1/2 to 4 quart (3.5 to 4 L) slow cooker.

Add remaining 3 ingredients. Stir. Cook, covered, on Low for 4 to 5 hours or on High for 2 to 2 1/2 hours. Makes about 7 cups (1.75 L).

1 cup (250 mL): 109 Calories; 1.2 g Total Fat (0.4 g Mono, 0.2 g Poly, 0.1 g Sat); 0 mg Cholesterol; 16 g Carbohydrate; 2 g Fibre; 3 g Protein; 553 mg Sodium

Note: If using portobello mushrooms, remove gills before chopping.

Easy Tomato Soup

This is a fresh, light-tasting tomato soup that couldn't be easier to make! Try serving this attractive red soup in white bowls for a striking contrast.

Tomato juice	12 cups	3 L
Granulated sugar	2 tbsp.	30 mL
Worcestershire sauce	1 tbsp.	15 mL
Italian seasoning	2 tsp.	10 mL
Lime juice	1 tbsp.	15 mL

Combine first 4 ingredients in 4 to 5 quart (4 to 5 L) slow cooker. Cook, covered, on Low for 5 to 6 hours or on High for 2 1/2 to 3 hours.

Add lime juice. Stir. Makes about 12 cups (3 L).

1 cup (250 mL): 91 Calories; 0.1 g Total Fat (trace Mono, 0.1 g Poly, trace Sat); trace Cholesterol; 23 g Carbohydrate; 1 g Fibre; 4 g Protein; 1329 mg Sodium

Pictured on page 35.

Paré Pointer
To take a peek, become a mountain climber.

Creamy Clam Chowder

Everyone's favourite seafood soup with five ingredients! This version is rich and creamy with the delicious flavours of potatoes, clams and dill.

Cans of minced clams (3 oz., 85 g, each), drained and liquid reserved	3	3
Can of condensed cream of mushroom and onion soup	10 oz.	284 mL
Diced peeled potato	3 cups	750 mL
Dried dillweed	1/2 tsp.	2 mL
Homogenized milk	1 1/2 cups	375 mL

Combine clam liquid, soup and 1 cup (250 mL) water in 3 1/2 to 4 quart (3.5 to 4 L) slow cooker. Stir until smooth. Chill clams.

Add potato and dill to slow cooker. Stir. Cook, covered, on Low for 6 to 8 hours or on High for 3 to 4 hours.

Add milk and reserved clams. Cook, covered, on High for about 15 minutes until heated through. Makes about 7 cups (1.75 L).

1 cup (250 mL): 185 Calories; 5.2 g Total Fat (0.5 g Mono, 0.2 g Poly, 2.0 g Sat); 38 mg Cholesterol; 26 g Carbohydrate; 2 g Fibre; 10 g Protein; 739 mg Sodium

Coconut Carrot Soup

Try this fragrant, velvety smooth soup with a splash of lime juice—any way you serve it, it's sweet, spicy and absolutely delicious.

Chopped onion	1 1/2 cups	375 mL
Thai red curry paste	2 tsp.	10 mL
Sliced carrot	6 cups	1.5 L
Prepared vegetable broth	5 cups	1.25 L
Can of coconut milk	14 oz.	398 mL

Heat large greased frying pan on medium. Add onion. Cook for about 8 minutes, stirring often, until onion is softened.

(continued on next page)

Add curry paste. Heat and stir for 1 minute. Transfer to 3 1/2 to 4 quart (3.5 to 4 L) slow cooker.

Add carrot, broth and a sprinkle of salt. Stir. Cook, covered, on Low for 8 to 10 hours or on High for 4 to 5 hours.

Add coconut milk. Stir. Carefully process with hand blender or in blender in batches until smooth (see Safety Tip). Makes about 10 cups (2.5 L).

1 cup (250 mL): 142 Calories; 9.6 g Total Fat (0.6 g Mono, 0.3 g Poly, 7.6 g Sat); 0 mg Cholesterol; 14 g Carbohydrate; 3 g Fibre; 2 g Protein; 383 mg Sodium

Safety Tip: Follow manufacturer's instructions for processing hot liquids.

Curry Corn Soup

This rich, smooth soup blends the lovely flavours of mild curry, sweet coconut and creamed corn.

Chopped onion	1 1/2 cups	375 mL
Hot curry paste	1 tbsp.	15 mL
Granulated sugar	1 tsp.	5 mL
Can of coconut milk	14 oz.	398 mL
Frozen kernel corn, thawed	4 cups	1 L

Heat large greased frying pan on medium. Add onion. Cook for about 8 minutes, stirring often, until softened.

Add curry paste and sugar. Heat and stir for 1 minute. Add coconut milk. Stir. Transfer to 4 to 5 quart (4 to 5 L) slow cooker.

Add corn, 2 cups (500 mL) water and a generous sprinkle of salt. Stir. Cook, covered, on Low for 5 to 6 hours or on High for 2 1/2 to 3 hours. Carefully process with hand blender or in blender in batches until smooth (see Safety Tip). Makes about 6 cups (1.5 L).

1 cup (250 mL): 244 Calories; 15.9 g Total Fat (1.1 g Mono, 0.4 g Poly, 12.7 g Sat); 0 mg Cholesterol; 24 g Carbohydrate; 4 g Fibre; 5 g Protein; 352 mg Sodium

Safety Tip: Follow manufacturer's instructions for processing hot liquids.

Cherry Beef Roast

This roast cooks up into a melt-in-your-mouth main course with a sweet and smoky sauce to drizzle over top.

Seasoned salt	1 tsp.	5 mL
Boneless beef cross-rib roast	3 1/2 lbs.	1.6 kg
Hickory barbecue sauce	1 cup	250 mL
Cherry jam	1/2 cup	125 mL
Prepared beef broth	1/2 cup	125 mL

Rub seasoned salt over roast. Heat large greased frying pan on medium-high. Add roast. Cook for about 8 minutes, turning occasionally, until browned on all sides. Transfer to 4 to 5 quart (4 to 5 L) slow cooker.

Stir remaining 3 ingredients in small bowl until smooth. Pour over roast. Cook, covered, on Low for 8 to 10 hours or on High for 4 to 5 hours. Transfer roast to cutting board. Cover with foil. Let stand for 10 minutes. Skim and discard fat from cooking liquid. Carefully process with hand blender or in blender in batches until smooth (see Safety Tip). Makes about 3 1/2 cups (875 mL) sauce. Slice roast and arrange on large serving plate. Serve with sauce. Serves 10.

1 serving with 5 1/2 tbsp (82 mL) sauce: 616 Calories; 42.0 g Total Fat (18.2 g Mono, 1.8 g Poly, 16.4 g Sat); 165 mg Cholesterol; 14 g Carbohydrate; trace Fibre; 43 g Protein; 515 mg Sodium

Safety Tip: Follow manufacturer's instructions for processing hot liquids.

1. Texas Chili, page 59
2. Steak and Veggie Dinner, page 70
3. Tender Beef With Lemon Parsley, page 64

Peppered Roast

For even better flavour, prepare this pot roast the day before.

Sliced onion	4 cups	1 L
Boneless beef blade (or cross-rib) roast	3 lbs.	1.4 kg
Can of tomato paste	5 1/2 oz.	156 mL
Soy sauce	1/4 cup	60 mL
Envelope of green peppercorn sauce mix	1 1/4 oz.	38 g

Put onion into 4 to 5 quart (4 to 5 L) slow cooker. Place roast over onion. Sprinkle generously with pepper.

Combine next 3 ingredients and 2 cups (500 mL) water in medium bowl. Pour over roast. Cook, covered, on High for 4 1/2 to 5 hours. Transfer roast to cutting board. Cover with foil. Let stand for 10 minutes. Skim and discard fat from sauce. Slice roast and arrange on large serving plate (see Note). Pour sauce over top. Serves 10.

1 serving: 523 Calories; 35.5 g Total Fat (15.2 g Mono, 1.3 g Poly, 14.0 g Sat); 142 mg Cholesterol; 11 g Carbohydrate; 2 g Fibre; 39 g Protein; 852 mg Sodium

Note: The cold roast slices very neatly, so chill the leftovers overnight before cutting. Pour some of the sauce into a casserole dish, arrange sliced beef over top and cover with remaining sauce. Reheat, covered, in 350°F (175°C) oven for about 45 minutes until hot.

1. Barbecued Pulled Pork, page 103
2. Pulled Chicken Fajitas, page 76
3. Unsloppy Joe Filling, page 66

Corned Beef and Winter Vegetables

This tender and flavourful corned beef brisket is slow cooked in apple cider with winter vegetables—perfect for a cozy autumn supper. Serve alongside boiled or mashed potatoes to complete the meal.

Corned beef brisket, rinsed and drained	2 1/2 lbs.	1.1 kg
Baby carrots	3 cups	750 mL
Chopped, peeled yellow turnip (rutabaga), 1 1/2 inch (3.8 cm) pieces	3 cups	750 mL
Sweet apple cider	3 cups	750 mL
Fresh (or frozen, thawed) Brussels sprouts, cut in half	3 cups	750 mL

Place brisket in 5 to 7 quart (5 to 7 L) slow cooker. Add carrots and turnip. Pour apple cider over top. Cook, covered, on High for 4 to 5 hours.

Add Brussels sprouts. Cook, covered, on High for about 30 minutes until Brussels sprouts are tender. Transfer brisket to cutting board. Cover with foil. Let stand for 10 minutes. Slice brisket across the grain. Transfer to large serving platter. Transfer vegetables with slotted spoon to serving bowl. Skim and discard fat from cooking liquid. Serve with vegetables and cooking liquid. Serves 8.

1 serving with 1/2 cup (125 mL) cooking liquid: 374 Calories; 21.3 g Total Fat (10.2 g Mono, 0.8 g Poly, 6.7 g Sat); 77 mg Cholesterol; 22 g Carbohydrate; 3 g Fibre; 23 g Protein; 1798 mg Sodium

Sandwich Brisket

Once this fork-tender beef brisket has cooled, slice it up for weekday sandwiches or freeze for later use. Heat the cooking liquid for dipping, or make gravy for hot beef sandwiches. Cooled brisket can also be julienned for stir-fries or salads.

Boneless beef brisket roast	4 lbs.	1.8 kg
Chopped onion	1 cup	250 mL
Garlic cloves, minced (or 3/4 tsp., 4 mL, powder)	3	3
Prepared beef broth	1 cup	250 mL
Red wine vinegar	1/4 cup	60 mL

Place brisket in 5 to 7 quart (5 to 7 L) slow cooker.

Heat medium greased frying pan on medium. Add onion and garlic. Cook, stirring often, for about 10 minutes, until starting to brown. Sprinkle generously with salt and pepper.

Add broth and vinegar to onion mixture. Bring to a boil. Pour over brisket. Cook, covered, on High for 4 1/2 to 5 hours until brisket is very tender. Remove brisket from slow cooker. Cool completely. Wrap in plastic wrap. Let stand in refrigerator for 6 hours or overnight. Chill cooking liquid. Remove and discard fat from brisket and cooking liquid. Makes about 1 1/4 cups (250 mL) cooking liquid. Slice brisket thinly. Serve brisket with cooking liquid. Makes about 2.2 lbs (1 kg) brisket.

3 oz. (85 g) portion with 1/4 cup (60 mL) cooking liquid: 203 Calories; 7.0 g Total Fat (3.0 g Mono, 0.4 g Poly, 2.5 g Sat); 64 mg Cholesterol; 2 g Carbohydrate; trace Fibre; 31 g Protein; 261 mg Sodium

Paré Pointer

Modern spiders have their own websites.

Tomato Paprikash

Tender, bite-sized beef pairs well with tomatoes and paprika in this rich, saucy dish. It can be served with boiled potatoes or spooned over egg noodles.

Chopped onion	1 1/2 cups	375 mL
Boneless beef blade steak, trimmed of fat, cut into 1 inch (2.5 cm) cubes	3 lbs.	1.4 kg
Can of diced tomatoes (with juice)	14 oz.	398 mL
Can of tomato paste	5 1/2 oz.	156 mL
Paprika	2 tbsp.	30 mL

Put onion into 4 to 5 quart (4 to 5 L) slow cooker. Arrange beef over top. Sprinkle generously with salt and pepper.

Combine remaining 3 ingredients, 1/2 cup (125 mL) water and a generous sprinkle of salt and pepper in medium bowl. Pour over beef. Cook, covered, on Low for 8 to 10 hours or on High for 4 to 5 hours. Makes about 8 cups (2 L).

3/4 cup (175 mL): 262 Calories; 13.8 g Total Fat (5.4 g Mono, 0.7 g Poly, 5.1 g Sat); 86 mg Cholesterol; 8 g Carbohydrate; 2 g Fibre; 26 g Protein; 433 mg Sodium

Meat Sauce for Many

When you make a meat sauce in the slow cooker, all that's left to do is cook up some noodles and toss a salad. Freeze in portions to save for pasta nights!

Lean ground beef	2 lbs.	900 g
Hot Italian sausage, casing removed	1 lb.	454 g
Sliced fresh white mushrooms	4 cups	1 L
Tomato pasta sauce	10 cups	2.5 L
Italian seasoning	2 tbsp.	30 mL

Scramble-fry ground beef and sausage in large greased frying pan on medium-high for about 10 minutes until no longer pink. Drain. Transfer to 4 to 5 quart (4 to 5 L) slow cooker.

Add mushrooms to same greased frying pan. Cook on medium-high for about 5 minutes until softened. Add to slow cooker.

(continued on next page)

Add pasta sauce and Italian seasoning. Stir well. Cook, covered, on Low for 6 to 8 hours or on High for 3 to 4 hours. Makes about 13 cups (3.25 L).

1/2 cup (125 mL): 136 Calories; 6.7 g Total Fat (1.3 g Mono, 0.4 g Poly, 2.3 g Sat); 28 mg Cholesterol; 10 g Carbohydrate; trace Fibre; 10 g Protein; 377 mg Sodium

---

Texas Chili

Forget ground beef—diced beef roast cooks up tender in the slow cooker for a real Texas-style chili, with lots of beans and tomatoes too. Increase the chili powder if you like a stronger-flavoured chili.

Boneless beef blade (or chuck) roast, cut into 1/2 inch (12 mm) pieces	3 lbs.	1.4 kg
Chopped onion	2 1/2 cups	625 mL
Cans of stewed tomatoes (14 oz., 398 mL, each), divided	3	3
Cans of red kidney beans (14 oz., 398 mL, each), rinsed and drained	3	3
Chili powder	2 tbsp.	30 mL

Heat large well-greased frying pan on medium-high. Cook beef, in 3 batches, for about 5 minutes, stirring occasionally, until browned. Transfer to 4 to 5 quart (4 to 5 L) slow cooker. Sprinkle generously with salt and pepper.

Add onion to same greased frying pan. Cook for about 5 minutes, stirring often, until softened. Add to slow cooker.

Process 2 cans of stewed tomatoes in blender or food processor until smooth. Add to slow cooker. Stir. Add remaining can of tomatoes, kidney beans and chili powder. Stir well. Cook, covered, on Low for 9 to 10 hours or on High for 4 1/2 to 5 hours. Makes about 12 cups (3 L).

1 cup (250 mL): 424 Calories; 21.1 g Total Fat (9.1 g Mono, 1.1 g Poly, 7.7 g Sat); 77 mg Cholesterol; 30 g Carbohydrate; 9 g Fibre; 28 g Protein; 371 mg Sodium

Pictured on page 53 and on back cover.

Stuffed Peppers

These colourful peppers are stuffed with savoury beef and rice—a pretty dish to serve for company. It cooks up with extra tomato sauce to spoon over the servings.

Large red peppers	4	4
Lean ground beef	1 lb.	454 g
Finely chopped onion	1/4 cup	60 mL
Cooked long-grain white rice (about 1/2 cup, 125 mL, uncooked)	1 1/2 cups	375 mL
Tomato and herb pasta sauce	3 cups	750 mL

Cut 1/2 inch (12 mm) from top of each pepper. Remove seeds and ribs. Trim bottom of each pepper so it will sit flat, being careful not to cut into cavity. Set aside. Discard stems from tops, dicing remaining pepper surrounding stem.

Scramble-fry beef, onion and diced pepper in large greased frying pan on medium for about 10 minutes until beef is no longer pink. Sprinkle with salt and pepper. Transfer to large bowl.

Add rice and 3/4 cup (175 mL) pasta sauce to beef mixture. Stir. Spoon into prepared peppers. Arrange stuffed peppers in 5 to 7 quart (5 to 7 L) slow cooker. Pour remaining pasta sauce over and around peppers. Cook, covered, on Low for 4 to 5 hours or on High for 2 to 2 1/2 hours. Serve sauce with peppers. Makes about 1 cup (250 mL) sauce and 4 peppers.

1 pepper with 1/4 cup (60 mL) sauce: 454 Calories; 18.4 g Total Fat (0.7 g Mono, 0.6 g Poly, 5.6 g Sat); 74 mg Cholesterol; 41 g Carbohydrate; 4 g Fibre; 29 g Protein; 1079 mg Sodium

Beer-Braised Pot Roast

This roast is tender and flavourful, and the sauce has molasses sweetness and a hint of horseradish. Serve slices over egg noodles with a side of mixed veggies.

Boneless beef cross-rib roast	4 lbs.	1.8 kg
Stout beer	1 1/4 cups	300 mL
Fancy (mild) molasses	1/4 cup	60 mL
Envelope of vegetable soup mix	1 1/4 oz.	40 g
Creamed horseradish	1 tbsp.	15 mL

Sprinkle roast generously with salt and pepper. Place in 4 to 5 quart (4 to 5 L) slow cooker.

Combine next 3 ingredients in small bowl. Pour over roast. Cook, covered, on High for 5 to 6 hours. Transfer roast to cutting board. Cover with foil. Let stand for 10 minutes. Skim and discard fat from cooking liquid. Carefully process in blender in batches (see Safety Tip). Transfer to medium bowl.

Add horseradish. Stir. Cut roast into thin slices. Transfer to large serving platter. Pour sauce over top. Serves 12.

1 serving: 383 Calories; 25.7 g Total Fat (11.0 g Mono, 0.9 g Poly, 10.2 g Sat); 102 mg Cholesterol; 8 g Carbohydrate; trace Fibre; 27 g Protein; 226 mg Sodium

Safety Tip: Follow manufacturer's instructions for processing hot liquids.

Curry Beef Stew

This beef cooks up into a satisfying main course flavoured with a spicy-sweet sauce.

Boneless beef blade (or chuck) roast, trimmed of fat, cut into 1 inch (2.5 cm) pieces	3 lbs.	1.4 kg
Prepared beef broth	1 1/2 cups	375 mL
Sweetened applesauce	1 1/2 cups	375 mL
Mixed dried fruit (such as raisins, apricot, apple and pineapple), chopped	1 cup	250 mL
Hot curry paste	2 tbsp.	30 mL

Heat large well-greased frying pan on medium-high. Cook beef, in 3 batches, for about 5 minutes, stirring occasionally, until browned. Transfer to 3 1/2 to 4 quart (3.5 to 4 L) slow cooker. Sprinkle generously with salt and pepper.

Add remaining 4 ingredients to same frying pan. Heat and stir for 1 minute, scraping any brown bits from bottom of pan. Pour over beef. Cook, covered, on Low for 6 to 8 hours or on High for 3 to 4 hours. Skim and discard fat. Makes about 7 cups (1.75 L).

3/4 cup (175 mL): 646 Calories; 41.6 g Total Fat (17.9 g Mono, 1.9 g Poly, 15.9 g Sat); 157 mg Cholesterol; 25 g Carbohydrate; 3 g Fibre; 42 g Protein; 588 mg Sodium

Taco Beef Hash

A one-dish meal with Mexican flair! It makes a satisfying brunch or lunch for the whole family.

Lean ground beef	1 lb.	454 g
Diced cooked potato	4 cups	1 L
Taco seasoning mix, stir before measuring	2 tbsp.	30 mL
Large eggs	6	6
Can of condensed cheddar cheese (or condensed cream of onion) soup	10 oz.	285 g

(continued on next page)

Scramble-fry ground beef in large greased frying pan on medium-high for about 5 minutes until no longer pink. Transfer to large bowl.

Add potato, taco seasoning and a generous sprinkle of pepper. Stir well. Transfer to well-greased 3 1/2 to 4 quart (3.5 to 4 L) slow cooker.

Whisk eggs and soup in medium bowl until smooth. Pour over beef mixture. Stir. Cook, covered, on High for about 2 hours until set. Serves 6.

1 serving: 346 Calories; 14.7 g Total Fat (0.5 g Mono, 0.3 g Poly, 5.5 g Sat); 268 mg Cholesterol; 28 g Carbohydrate; 3 g Fibre; 24 g Protein; 1077 mg Sodium

Variation: To spice up this dish, replace taco seasoning with 2 tsp. (10 mL) finely chopped chipotle peppers in adobo sauce (see Tip, page 41). Add a generous sprinkle of salt to the potato mixture.

Onion Pepper Swiss Steak

Serve up steak with tangy tomatoes for a weekend supper for the family. Serve with garlic mashed potatoes or your favourite pasta.

Boneless beef blade steaks, trimmed of fat, cut into 4 pieces	1 1/2 lbs.	680 g
All-purpose flour	3 tbsp.	50 mL
Thinly sliced onion	2 cups	500 mL
Thinly sliced green pepper	1 3/4 cups	425 mL
Can of diced tomatoes (with juice)	14 oz.	398 mL

Sprinkle steaks with salt and pepper. Press into flour in small shallow dish until coated on all sides. Heat large greased frying pan on medium-high. Add steaks. Cook for about 2 minutes per side until browned. Transfer to 3 1/2 to 4 quart (3.5 to 4 L) slow cooker.

Add next 3 ingredients and a sprinkle of salt and pepper. Cook, covered, on Low for 6 to 7 hours or on High for 3 to 3 1/2 hours. Transfer to serving platter. Serves 4.

1 serving: 378 Calories; 19.2 g Total Fat (7.7 g Mono, 1.2 g Poly, 6.8 g Sat); 112 mg Cholesterol; 16 g Carbohydrate; 2 g Fibre; 35 g Protein; 690 mg Sodium

Tender Beef With Lemon Parsley

Our simplified version of traditional gremolata—*a fresh parsley and lemon mixture—adds freshness to melt-in-your-mouth beef stew. This is excellent over rice or noodles.*

Medium lemons	2	2
Chopped fresh parsley	1/2 cup	125 mL
Sliced onion	2 cups	500 mL
Boneless beef blade (or cross-rib) roast, cut into 1 1/2 inch (3.8 cm) pieces	2 1/2 lbs.	1.1 kg
Roasted garlic tomato pasta sauce	3 cups	750 mL

Grate 1 tbsp. (15 mL) lemon zest into small bowl. Add parsley. Stir. Chill, covered.

Put onion and into 3 1/2 to 4 quart (3.5 to 4 L) slow cooker. Sprinkle generously with salt and pepper.

Heat large well-greased frying pan on medium-high. Cook beef, in 2 batches, for about 5 minutes, stirring occasionally, until browned. Transfer to slow cooker.

Squeeze 1/3 cup (75 mL) lemon juice into medium bowl. Add pasta sauce and 1/2 cup (125 mL) water. Stir. Pour over beef. Stir well. Cook, covered, on Low for 8 to 10 hours or on High for 4 to 5 hours. Skim and discard fat. Stir. Sprinkle with parsley mixture. Makes about 7 1/2 cups (1.9 L).

3/4 cup (175 mL): 315 Calories; 21.1 g Total Fat (9.4 g Mono, 1.2 g Poly, 7.8 g Sat); 77 mg Cholesterol; 9 g Carbohydrate; 2 g Fibre; 21 g Protein; 382 mg Sodium

Pictured on page 53 and on back cover.

Rouladen

These tender beef and bacon rolls are bursting with smoky flavour for guest-worthy holiday fare. The mild, tasty gravy would be wonderful served over mashed or boiled potatoes.

Beef rouladen steaks, 1/4 inch (6 mm) thick	8	8
Prepared horseradish	3 tbsp.	50 mL
Bacon slices	8	8
Envelope of onion soup mix	1 1/2 oz.	42 g
Minute tapioca	2 tbsp.	30 mL

Arrange steaks on work surface. Spread about 1 tsp. (5 mL) horseradish over each steak. Sprinkle with pepper. Place 1 strip of bacon on each steak. Starting at one short end, roll to enclose filling. Arrange beef rolls, seam-side down, in single layer in 4 to 5 quart (4 to 5 L) slow cooker.

Combine soup mix, minute tapioca and 2 cups (500 mL) water in small bowl. Pour over beef. Do not stir. Cook, covered, on Low for 8 to 9 hours or on High for 4 to 4 1/2 hours. Transfer rolls with slotted spoon to large serving platter. Cover to keep warm. Skim and discard fat from cooking liquid. Carefully process in blender in batches until smooth (see Safety Tip). Pour sauce over rolls. Serves 8.

1 serving: 240 Calories; 7.4 g Total Fat (3.1 g Mono, 0.5 g Poly, 2.5 g Sat); 87 mg Cholesterol; 6 g Carbohydrate; trace Fibre; 35 g Protein; 686 mg Sodium

Safety Tip: Follow manufacturer's instructions for processing hot liquids.

Paré Pointer

When robots wash their hands, they have to dry carefully to avoid rusty nails.

Luau Meatballs

These sweet-and-sour meatballs are smothered in a tasty pineapple and green pepper sauce. Thaw the meatballs overnight in the refrigerator and then assemble in the morning. The final stage of cooking will give you just enough time to steam up some rice before dinner!

Box of frozen cooked meatballs, thawed	2 lbs.	900 g
Cans of crushed pineapple (with juice), 14 oz., 398 mL, each	2	2
Thick teriyaki basting sauce	2/3 cup	150 mL
Cornstarch	3 tbsp.	50 mL
Diced green pepper	1 1/2 cups	375 mL

Put meatballs into 4 to 5 quart (4 to 5 L) slow cooker.

Combine pineapple, teriyaki sauce, 1/3 cup (75 mL) water and a sprinkle of pepper in medium bowl. Pour over meatballs. Cook, covered, on Low for 6 to 8 hours or on High for 3 to 4 hours.

Stir 1/3 cup (75 mL) water into cornstarch in small bowl until smooth. Pour over meatballs. Add green pepper. Stir well. Cook, covered, on High for about 20 minutes until boiling and thickened. Makes about 9 cups (2.25 L).

1 cup (250 mL): 418 Calories; 23.8 g Total Fat (trace Mono, 0.1 g Poly, 10.0 g Sat); 47 mg Cholesterol; 33 g Carbohydrate; 4 g Fibre; 6 g Protein; 1370 mg Sodium

Unsloppy Joe Filling

This favourite bun filling has a sweet, mellow tomato flavour, and oats to hold the meaty mixture together for minimal mess—ideal for kids! Easy to freeze in smaller portions for a hot lunch or supper in a hurry.

Lean ground beef	3 lbs.	1.4 kg
Finely chopped onion	1 cup	250 mL
Cans of condensed tomato soup (10 oz., 284 mL, each)	2	2
Ketchup	2 1/2 cups	625 mL
Quick-cooking rolled oats	1 cup	250 mL

(continued on next page)

Scramble-fry ground beef and onion in large greased frying pan on medium-high for about 10 minutes until no longer pink. Transfer to 3 1/2 to 4 quart (3.5 to 4 L) slow cooker.

Add soup and ketchup. Stir. Cook, covered, on Low for 5 to 6 hours or on High for 2 1/2 to 3 hours.

Add oats. Stir well. Cook, covered, on High for about 20 minutes until thickened. Makes about 9 cups (2.25 L).

1/2 cup (125 mL): 236 Calories; 8.2 g Total Fat (0.2 g Mono, 0.1 g Poly, 3.1 g Sat); 49 mg Cholesterol; 25 g Carbohydrate; 1 g Fibre; 16 g Protein; 478 mg Sodium

Pictured on page 54.

Falafel Meatloaf Pie

This is classic meatloaf with a Mediterranean makeover, served with tangy tzatziki. Use leftovers for delicious gyro sandwiches or wraps.

Lean ground beef	1 1/2 lbs.	680 g
Large egg, fork-beaten	1	1
Box of falafel mix	10 oz.	285 g
Chili paste (sambal oelek)	2 tsp.	10 mL
Tzatziki, divided	1 1/2 cups	375 mL

Scramble-fry ground beef in large greased frying pan on medium-high for about 5 minutes until no longer pink. Transfer to large bowl.

Add next 3 ingredients, 1/2 cup (125 mL) tzatziki and 3/4 cup (175 mL) water. Mix well. Press evenly into greased 8 inch (20 cm) springform pan. Put an even layer (2 to 3 inches, 5 to 7.5 cm, thick) of crumpled foil into bottom of 5 to 7 quart (5 to 7 L) slow cooker (see Tip, page 80). Pour 2 cups (500 mL) boiling water into slow cooker. Place pan over foil, pushing down gently to settle evenly. Cook, covered, on Low for 5 to 6 hours or on High for 2 1/2 to 3 hours until centre is firm. Remove pan from slow cooker. Let stand on wire rack for 10 minutes. Serve with remaining tzatziki. Cuts into 8 wedges.

1 wedge with 2 tbsp. (30 mL) tzatziki: 328 Calories; 15.5 g Total Fat (0.3 g Mono, 0.2 g Poly, 5.2 g Sat); 82 mg Cholesterol; 24 g Carbohydrate; 2 g Fibre; 24 g Protein; 626 mg Sodium

Mushroom Beef Sauce

Use a combination of your favourite mushrooms in this succulent beef and red wine sauce. The results are delicious and versatile—serve over potatoes, rice or pasta for a complete meal, and garnish with chopped fresh parsley.

Stewing beef, trimmed of fat, cut into 1 inch (2.5 cm) cubes	2 lbs.	900 g
Envelope of mushroom pasta sauce mix	1 1/4 oz.	38 g
Butter (or hard margarine)	1 tbsp.	15 mL
Sliced fresh mixed mushrooms	4 cups	1 L
Dry (or alcohol-free) red wine	3/4 cup	175 mL

Combine beef and sauce mix in 4 to 5 quart (4 to 5 L) slow cooker.

Melt butter in large frying pan on medium. Add mushrooms. Cook for about 8 minutes, stirring often, until browned. Transfer to slow cooker.

Add wine and 3/4 cup (175 mL) water. Cook, covered, on Low for 8 to 9 hours or on High for 4 to 4 1/2 hours. Skim and discard fat. Makes about 5 1/2 cups (1.4 L).

1/2 cup (125 mL): 194 Calories; 11.8 g Total Fat (4.8 g Mono, 0.4 g Poly, 4.7 g Sat); 53 mg Cholesterol; 3 g Carbohydrate; trace Fibre; 15 g Protein; 203 mg Sodium

Beefy Mac and Cheese

This is an easy, family-friendly pasta dish with lots of cheesy flavour. Sprinkle with Parmesan cheese or chili flakes and serve with garlic bread.

Lean ground beef	1 lb.	454 g
Chopped onion	1 cup	250 mL
Cooked elbow macaroni (about 1 3/4 cups, 425 mL, uncooked)	4 cups	1 L
Tomato basil pasta sauce	3 cups	750 mL
Grated Cheddar cheese	2 cups	500 mL

Scramble-fry ground beef and onion in large greased frying pan on medium for about 10 minutes until beef is no longer pink. Sprinkle with salt and pepper. Transfer to greased 3 1/2 to 4 quart (3.5 to 4 L) slow cooker.

(continued on next page)

Add remaining 3 ingredients and 1/2 cup (125 mL) water. Stir. Cook, covered, on Low for 3 to 4 hours or on High for 1 1/2 to 2 hours until heated through and cheese is melted. Makes about 8 cups (2 L).

1 cup (250 mL): 381 Calories; 18.0 g Total Fat (3.0 g Mono, 0.4 g Poly, 8.3 g Sat); 67 mg Cholesterol; 29 g Carbohydrate; 1 g Fibre; 24 g Protein; 639 mg Sodium

Peppered Beef Dip

Beef au jus is a great trade-up from the usual lunchtime fare, and you'll get a hands-on meal out of this classic diner favourite! Add onions, peppers and cheese for a Philly cheese steak.

Boneless beef blade (or chuck) roast	3 lbs.	1.4 kg
Pepper	1 tbsp.	15 mL
Can of condensed beef broth	10 oz.	284 mL
Can of condensed onion soup	10 oz.	284 mL
Panini buns, split	6	6

Sprinkle roast with pepper. Heat large greased frying pan on medium-high. Add roast. Cook for about 8 minutes, turning occasionally, until browned on all sides. Transfer to 4 to 5 quart (4 to 5 L) slow cooker.

Add broth and soup to same frying pan. Heat and stir, scraping any brown bits from bottom of pan, until boiling. Pour over roast. Cook, covered, on Low for 8 to 9 hours or on High for 4 to 4 1/2 hours. Transfer roast to cutting board. Cover with foil. Let stand for 10 minutes. Skim and discard fat from cooking liquid. Carefully process in blender until smooth (see Safety Tip). Makes about 2 1/2 cups (625 mL) cooking liquid. Cut roast into thin slices.

Fill buns with beef. Cut each bun in half. Serve with small bowl of cooking liquid for dipping. Makes 12 sandwiches.

1 sandwich with 3 tbsp (50 mL) cooking liquid: 395 Calories; 21.3 g Total Fat (8.6 g Mono, 0.9 g Poly, 7.6 g Sat); 77 mg Cholesterol; 24 g Carbohydrate; 2 g Fibre; 26 g Protein; 653 mg Sodium

Safety Tip: Follow manufacturer's instructions for processing hot liquids.

Steak and Veggie Dinner

On busy autumn days, make this all-in-one comfort dish in the slow cooker. A little salt and pepper is all you need to season this flavourful, family-friendly meal. Serve with crusty bread to mop up the sauce.

Unpeeled red potatoes, cut into 2 inch (5 cm) pieces	2 1/2 lbs.	1.1 kg
Sliced carrot (1 1/2 inch, 3.8 cm, thick)	2 1/2 cups	625 mL
Boneless beef blade steak, cut into 6 pieces	2 lbs.	900 g
Chopped onion	2 cups	500 mL
Can of Italian-style stewed tomatoes, cut up	19 oz.	540 mL

Combine potatoes and carrot in 5 to 7 quart (5 to 7 L) slow cooker.

Heat large well-greased frying pan on medium-high. Add beef. Cook for about 2 minutes per side until browned. Transfer to slow cooker.

Add onion to same greased frying pan. Cook for about 5 minutes, stirring often, until softened. Add to beef. Sprinkle generously with salt and pepper.

Pour tomatoes over top. Cook, covered, on Low for 9 to 10 hours or on High for 4 1/2 to 5 hours. Serves 6.

1 serving: *495 Calories; 19.4 g Total Fat (8.1 g Mono, 1.8 g Poly, 6.3 g Sat); 100 mg Cholesterol; 45 g Carbohydrate; 7 g Fibre; 34 g Protein; 664 mg Sodium*

Pictured on page 53 and on back cover.

1. Red-Peppered Chorizo, page 24
2. Smokin' Smokies, page 23
3. Pork and Guacamole Tostadas, page 13

Thai Red Curry Beef

This rich, mildly-spiced coconut curry features tender beef and baby potatoes.
Spoon some of the sauce over rice, or dunk in some naan bread.

Baby potatoes, cut in half	2 lbs.	900 g
Boneless beef round steak, trimmed of fat, cut into 1 inch (2.5 cm) cubes	2 lbs.	900 g
Chopped sweet onion	2 cups	500 mL
Thai red curry paste	2 tbsp.	30 mL
Can of coconut milk	14 oz.	398 mL

Put potatoes into 4 to 5 quart (4 to 5 L) slow cooker.

Heat large well-greased frying pan on medium-high. Cook beef, in 2 batches, for about 10 minutes, stirring occasionally, until browned. Transfer to slow cooker. Sprinkle generously with salt and pepper.

Add onion to same greased frying pan. Reduce heat to medium. Cook for about 10 minutes, stirring occasionally, until starting to brown.

Add curry paste and 1 cup (250 mL) water. Heat and stir, scraping to remove any brown bits from bottom of pan, until boiling. Pour over beef. Cook, covered, on Low for 8 to 9 hours or on High for 4 to 4 1/2 hours.

Add coconut milk and a generous sprinkle of salt. Stir. Cook, covered, on High for 15 minutes. Makes about 8 cups (2 L).

1 cup (250 mL): 381 Calories; 17.3 g Total Fat (3.2 g Mono, 0.9 g Poly, 11.0 g Sat); 64 mg Cholesterol; 26 g Carbohydrate; 2 g Fibre; 30 g Protein; 472 mg Sodium

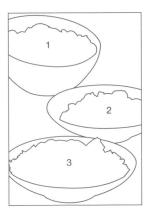

1. Chicken Stew, page 91
2. Cajun Turkey Stew, page 86
3. Pineapple Chicken, page 82

Sweet Mustard Roast Beef

Nothing beats a hearty roast beef and veggie dinner—and when you use the slow cooker, this comfort meal is easy too! Add a tossed salad and dinner is ready.

Sliced onion	2 cups	500 mL
Chopped carrot	2 cups	500 mL
Boneless beef blade (or chuck) roast	3 lbs.	1.4 kg
Dijon mustard	1/3 cup	75 mL
Fancy (mild) molasses	3 tbsp.	50 mL

Put onion into greased 5 to 7 quart (5 to 7 L) slow cooker. Scatter carrot over onion. Pour 1/2 cup (125 mL) water over top.

Sprinkle roast with salt and pepper. Heat large greased frying pan on medium-high. Add roast. Cook for about 8 minutes, turning occasionally, until browned on all sides.

Combine mustard and molasses in small bowl. Brush over roast. Place roast over carrots. Cook, covered, on Low for 8 to 10 hours or on High for 4 to 5 hours. Transfer roast to work surface. Cover with foil. Let stand for 10 minutes. Cut into slices. Transfer vegetables with slotted spoon to serving bowl. Skim and discard fat from cooking liquid. Makes 4 cups (1 L) cooking liquid. Serve with beef and vegetables. Serves 10.

1 serving with 6 tbsp (100 mL) cooking liquid: 350 Calories; 23.4 g Total Fat (10.2 g Mono, 1.0 g Poly, 9.1 g Sat); 92 mg Cholesterol; 9 g Carbohydrate; 1 g Fibre; 24 g Protein; 240 mg Sodium

Paré Pointer

You know why hummingbirds hum? They can't remember the words.

Florentine Chicken Lasagna

This colourful, well-layered lasagna has healthy, delicious ingredients like spinach and lean chicken paired with rich tomato and cheese flavour.

Lean ground chicken (or turkey)	1 lb.	454 g
Tomato cheese pasta sauce	4 cups	1 L
Grated Italian cheese blend	2 cups	500 mL
Oven-ready lasagna noodles, broken in half	9	9
Boxes of frozen chopped spinach (10 oz., 300 g, each), thawed, squeezed dry	2	2

Scramble-fry chicken in large greased frying pan on medium-high for about 5 minutes until no longer pink.

Add pasta sauce and 1/2 cup (125 mL) water. Stir.

To assemble, layer ingredients in greased 5 to 7 quart (5 to 7 L) slow cooker as follows:

1. 1 1/4 cups (300 mL) chicken mixture
2. 1/4 cup (60 mL) cheese
3. 6 lasagna noodle halves
4. 1/3 spinach
5. 1 1/4 cups (300 mL) chicken mixture
6. 1/4 cup (60 mL) cheese

Repeat steps 3, 4, 5 and 6 twice to make another 2 layers. Top with remainig cheese. Cook, covered, on Low for 4 to 5 hours or on High for 2 to 2 1/2 hours. Let stand, uncovered, for 10 minutes. Serves 6.

1 serving: 489 Calories; 20.9 g Total Fat (0.4 g Mono, 0.2 g Poly, 7.1 g Sat); 77 mg Cholesterol; 48 g Carbohydrate; 5 g Fibre; 31 g Protein; 1265 mg Sodium

Pictured on front cover.

Pulled Chicken Fajitas

Pulled chicken, salsa and tortilla wraps are delicious on their own, but can easily be made more elaborate—add shredded lettuce, sour cream, guacamole, cheese, sliced green onion or jalapeño.

Boneless, skinless chicken breast halves	1 1/2 lbs.	680 g
Taco seasoning mix, stir before measuring	2 tbsp.	30 mL
Chunky salsa, divided	2 cups	500 mL
Thinly sliced mixed peppers	2 cups	500 mL
Flour tortillas (9 inch, 22 cm, diameter)	8	8

Put chicken into 3 1/2 to 4 quart (3.5 to 4 L) slow cooker. Sprinkle with seasoning mix. Pour 1 1/2 cups (375 mL) salsa over top. Cook, covered, on Low for 6 to 7 hours or on High for 3 to 3 1/2 hours. Transfer chicken to large plate. Shred with 2 forks. Return to slow cooker.

Add peppers and remaining salsa. Stir. Cook, covered, on High for about 30 minutes until peppers are tender-crisp.

Spoon about 3/4 cup (175 mL) chicken mixture down centre of each tortilla. Fold bottom end of tortilla over filling. Fold in sides, leaving top end open. Makes 8 fajitas.

1 fajita: 266 Calories; 6.7 g Total Fat (0.9 g Mono, 0.6 g Poly, 1.7 g Sat); 50 mg Cholesterol; 31 g Carbohydrate; 1 g Fibre; 22 g Protein; 926 mg Sodium

Pictured on page 54.

Saucy Beans and Chicken

A can of beans, a few slices of bacon and some chicken thighs are all you need for this delicious, all-in-one meal—perfect for when you're hosting a crowd for the playoffs!

Chopped onion	1 cup	250 mL
Bacon slices, diced	3	3
Bone-in chicken thighs, skin removed	3 lbs.	1.4 kg
Can of baked beans in tomato sauce	14 oz.	398 mL
Grated Cheddar cheese	1/2 cup	125 mL

(continued on next page)

Heat large frying pan on medium-high. Add onion and bacon. Cook for about 5 minutes, stirring often, until onion is softened. Transfer with slotted spoon to 4 to 5 quart (4 to 5 L) slow cooker.

Add chicken to same frying pan. Sprinkle with salt and pepper. Cook on medium-high for about 3 minutes per side until browned. Transfer to slow cooker. Cook, covered, on Low for 6 to 7 hours or on High for 3 to 3 1/2 hours. Transfer chicken with slotted spoon to medium bowl. Skim and discard fat from cooking liquid.

Add beans and cheese. Stir. Return chicken to slow cooker. Cook, covered, on High for about 15 minutes until heated through. Serves 4.

1 serving: 579 Calories; 27.9 g Total Fat (10.4 g Mono, 5.2 g Poly, 9.2 g Sat); 192 mg Cholesterol; 23 g Carbohydrate; 5 g Fibre; 56 g Protein; 869 mg Sodium

Chicken Seafood Paella

Mildly spiced with smoked paprika, this paella's (pie-AY-yuh) combination of rice, chicken and seafood is a great introduction to the wonderful world of Spanish cuisine.

Boneless, skinless chicken thighs, halved	1 lb.	454 g
Smoked sweet paprika	3/4 tsp.	4 mL
Package of Spanish-style rice mix	14 oz.	397 g
Frozen seafood medley, thawed	1/2 lb.	340 g
Frozen peas, thawed	1 cup	250 mL

Heat large greased frying pan on medium-high. Add chicken. Sprinkle with paprika, salt and pepper. Cook for about 3 minutes per side until browned. Transfer to 3 1/2 to 4 quart (3.5 to 4 L) slow cooker.

Add rice mix and 3 1/2 cups (875 mL) water to slow cooker. Stir. Cook, covered, on Low for 6 to 7 hours or on High for 3 to 3 1/2 hours.

Add seafood and peas. Stir gently. Cook, covered, on High for about 20 minutes until seafood is cooked. Makes about 8 1/2 cups (2.1 L).

1 cup (250 mL): 162 Calories; 5.6 g Total Fat (2.2 g Mono, 1.4 g Poly, 1.4 g Sat); 86 mg Cholesterol; 11 g Carbohydrate; 2 g Fibre; 17 g Protein; 274 mg Sodium

Greek Lemon Drumettes

Savour the flavours of the Mediterranean with the fresh Parmesan, lemon and herb coating on these drumettes. Serve with fresh lemon wedges for an extra squeeze of citrus flavour.

Lemon yogurt	3/4 cup	175 mL
Chicken drumettes	3 lbs.	1.4 kg
Grated Parmesan cheese	1 1/2 cups	375 mL
Fine dry bread crumbs	1/2 cup	125 mL
Greek seasoning	2 tsp.	10 mL

Measure yogurt into large bowl. Add drumettes. Stir until coated.

Combine remaining 3 ingredients and a sprinkle of salt and pepper in large resealable freezer bag. Add 1/3 of drumettes. Seal bag. Toss until coated. Repeat with remaining drumettes. Put drumettes into greased 3 1/2 to 4 quart (3.5 to 4 L) slow cooker. Cook, covered, on Low for 8 to 9 hours or High for 4 to 4 1/2 hours. Makes about 24 drumettes.

1 drumette: 173 Calories; 11.5 g Total Fat (trace Mono, trace Poly, 3.9 g Sat); 50 mg Cholesterol; 3 g Carbohydrate; trace Fibre; 14 g Protein; 217 mg Sodium

Slow Cooker Turkey Dinner

Treat your family to their favourite holiday flavours any time of the year with this festive dish of turkey and vegetables in a creamy sauce, with lots of crispy stuffing on top.

Baby potatoes, cut in half	1 lb.	454 g
Boneless, skinless turkey thighs (or breasts), cut into 1 1/2 inch (3.8 cm) pieces	1 1/2 lbs.	680 g
Frozen mixed vegetables, thawed	4 cups	1 L
Can of condensed cream of celery soup	10 oz.	284 mL
Box of turkey cranberry stuffing mix	4 1/2 oz.	120 g

Layer first 3 ingredients, in order given, in greased 3 1/2 to 4 quart (3.5 to 4 L) slow cooker.

(continued on next page)

Whisk soup in small bowl until smooth. Spoon over vegetables.

Stir stuffing mix and 1/2 cup (125 mL) hot water in same small bowl until moistened. Spoon over turkey mixture. Cook, covered, on Low for 8 to 9 hours or on High for 4 to 4 1/2 hours. Serves 6.

1 serving: 369 Calories; 7.4 g Total Fat (0.1 g Mono, 0.2 g Poly, 2.4 g Sat); 79 mg Cholesterol; 39 g Carbohydrate; 3 g Fibre; 34 g Protein; 904 mg Sodium

Layered Turkey Enchilada

Layering this delicious Mexican entree is the key to its success. It's just as easy to make as lasagna (and as tasty!). It makes a big batch—perfect to feed a crowd.

Extra-lean ground turkey	3 lbs.	1.4 kg
Salsa	1 1/2 cups	375 mL
Can of condensed cream of chicken soup	10 oz.	284 mL
Flour tortillas (9 inch, 22 cm, diameter), cut or torn into eighths	6	6
Grated Mexican cheese blend	3 cups	750 mL

Scramble-fry turkey in greased Dutch oven on medium for about 15 minutes until no longer pink. Add salsa, soup and 1 1/2 cups (375 mL) water. Sprinkle generously with pepper. Stir.

To assemble, layer ingredients in greased 5 to 7 quart (5 to 7 L) slow cooker as follows:

1. 1/6 of turkey mixture
2. 8 tortilla pieces, overlapping
3. 1/6 of turkey mixture
4. 1/2 cup (125 mL) cheese

Repeat steps 2, 3 and 4 four more times to make another 4 layers. Cook, covered, on Low for 7 to 8 hours or on High for 3 1/2 to 4 hours. Let stand, uncovered, for 10 minutes. Makes about 12 cups (3 L).

1 cup (250 mL): 362 Calories; 19.9 g Total Fat (0.6 g Mono, 0.6 g Poly, 7.9 g Sat); 92 mg Cholesterol; 15 g Carbohydrate; trace Fibre; 30 g Protein; 726 mg Sodium

Tri-Colour Turkey Roll

Serve with a light yet rich-tasting cream sauce and an attractive garnish of fresh basil. Cooking with the skin on helps to keep the turkey breast moist.

Fresh spinach leaves, lightly packed	10 cups	2.5 L
Boneless, skin-on turkey breast roast (about 2 1/2 lbs., 1.1 kg)	1	1
Sun-dried tomato pesto, divided	9 tbsp.	150 mL
Grated Asiago cheese	3/4 cup	175 mL
Onion and chive cream cheese	1/2 cup	125 mL

Heat large greased frying pan on medium. Add spinach. Heat and stir until spinach is wilted. Cool.

To butterfly roast, cut horizontally lengthwise almost, but not quite, through to other side. Open flat. Place between 2 sheets of plastic wrap. Pound with mallet or rolling pin to 1/2 inch (12 mm) thickness. Spread 8 tbsp. (130 mL) pesto over roast. Arrange spinach over pesto. Sprinkle with Asiago cheese and pepper. Roll up from skinless short edge to enclose filling, making sure the skin is over top. Tie with butcher's string. Put an even layer (2 to 3 inches, 5 to 7.5 cm, thick) of crumpled foil into bottom of 5 to 7 quart (5 to 7 L) slow cooker (see Tip, below). Pour 1 cup (250 mL) boiling water into slow cooker. Place roast on foil. Cook, covered, on High for about 3 hours until internal temperature reaches 170°F (77°C). Transfer roast to cutting board. Cover with foil. Let stand for 10 minutes. Remove and discard string and skin from roast. Cut into 10 slices.

Carefully remove crumpled foil from slow cooker. Skim and discard fat from cooking liquid. Add cream cheese and remaining pesto. Whisk until smooth. Makes about 2 1/4 cup (550 mL) sauce. Serve sauce with turkey. Serves 10.

1 serving with 3 tbsp (50 mL) sauce: 239 Calories; 6.9 g Total Fat (0.3 g Mono, 0.2 g Poly, 3.4 g Sat); 99 mg Cholesterol; 11 g Carbohydrate; 2 g Fibre; 33 g Protein; 1404 mg Sodium

Pictured on page 89.

tip   Instead of using crumpled foil to elevate pans and other items, you can use canning jar lids or a roasting rack that fits your slow cooker if you have one.

Chicken Pesto Lasagna

Make this rich, cheesy lasagna for Italian night and serve with a green salad and toasty garlic bread. Customize the flavour by using your favourite pasta sauce!

Chopped cooked chicken	3 cups	750 mL
Basil pesto	1/4 cup	60 mL
Tomato pasta sauce	4 cups	1 L
Cooked lasagna noodles	9	9
Grated Italian cheese blend	4 cups	1 L

Combine chicken and pesto in medium bowl.

To assemble, layer ingredients in greased 5 to 7 quart (5 to 7 L) slow cooker as follows:

1. 1 cup (250 mL) pasta sauce
2. 3 lasagna noodles
3. 1 cup (250 mL) chicken mixture
4. 1 cup (250 mL) cheese
5. 1 cup (250 mL) pasta sauce
6. 3 lasagna noodles
7. 1 cup (250 mL) chicken mixture
8. 1 cup (250 mL) cheese
9. 1 cup (250 mL) pasta sauce
10. Remaining lasagna noodles
11. Remaining chicken mixture
12. Remaining pasta sauce
13. Remaining cheese

Cook, covered, on Low for 4 to 5 hours or on High for 2 to 2 1/2 hours until heated through. Let stand, uncovered, for 10 minutes. Serves 6.

1 serving: 648 Calories; 34.0 g Total Fat (2.3 g Mono, 1.5 g Poly, 13 g Sat); 122 mg Cholesterol; 36 g Carbohydrate; 1 g Fibre; 48 g Protein; 1312 mg Sodium

Chicken Siciliana

Olives and capers intensify the flavours of this sauce rich with chicken and eggplant. Sicily traditionally specializes in tube-shaped pasta, so serve with tubetti, macaroni or penne for an authentic touch.

Boneless, skinless chicken thighs, quartered	1 1/2 lbs.	680 g
Balsamic vinegar	2 tbsp.	30 mL
Chopped peeled eggplant (1/2 inch, 12 mm, pieces)	4 cups	1 L
Spicy tomato pasta sauce	3 cups	750 mL
Black olive tapenade	1/4 cup	60 mL

Heat large greased frying pan on medium-high. Add chicken. Cook for 3 minutes per side until browned. Add balsamic vinegar. Stir. Transfer to 3 1/2 to 4 quart (3.5 to 4 L) slow cooker.

Add eggplant and tomato sauce. Stir. Cook, covered, on Low for 8 to 10 hours or on High for 4 to 5 hours.

Add tapenade. Stir. Makes about 7 cups (1.75 L).

1 cup (250 mL): 212 Calories; 9.6 g Total Fat (3.2 g Mono, 1.9 g Poly, 2.2 g Sat); 64 mg Cholesterol; 11 g Carbohydrate; 2 g Fibre; 20 g Protein; 748 mg Sodium

Pineapple Chicken

This sweet and saucy chicken dish can be served over steamed rice with a simple veggie stir-fry.

Boneless, skinless chicken thighs, quartered	1 1/2 lbs.	680 g
Can of pineapple tidbits (with juice)	19 oz.	540 mL
Thinly sliced carrot	2 cups	500 mL
Thick teriyaki basting sauce	1/2 cup	125 mL
Cornstarch	1 1/2 tbsp.	25 mL

Heat large greased frying pan on medium-high. Add chicken. Cook for 3 minutes per side until browned. Transfer to 3 1/2 to 4 quart (3.5 to 4 L) slow cooker.

(continued on next page)

Add pineapple to same frying pan. Heat and stir until boiling. Add to slow cooker.

Add carrot and teriyaki sauce to slow cooker. Stir. Cook, covered, on Low for 6 to 7 hours or on High for 3 to 3 1/2 hours.

Stir 2 tbsp. (30 mL) water into cornstarch in small cup until smooth. Add to chicken mixture. Stir. Cook, covered, on High for about 10 minutes until sauce is slightly thickened. Makes about 6 cups (1.5 L).

1 cup (250 mL): 268 Calories; 9.4 g Total Fat (3.7 g Mono, 2.2 g Poly, 2.4 g Sat); 74 mg Cholesterol; 25 g Carbohydrate; 2 g Fibre; 21 g Protein; 646 mg Sodium

Pictured on page 72

Turkey and Wild Rice

This filling dish combines earthy wild rice and tender turkey pieces in a creamy sauce. Serve with a fresh veggie side like steamed asparagus.

Bacon slices, diced	3	3
Boneless, skinless turkey thighs, cut into 1 inch (2.5 cm) pieces	1 lb.	454 g
Can of condensed cream of wild mushroom soup	10 oz.	284 mL
Prepared chicken broth	1 cup	250 mL
Wild rice	1 cup	250 mL

Cook bacon in large frying pan on medium until crisp. Transfer with slotted spoon to paper towel-lined plate to drain. Drain and discard all but 1 tbsp. (15 mL) drippings.

Add turkey to same frying pan. Cook for about 10 minutes, stirring occasionally, until browned. Transfer to 3 1/2 to 4 quart (3.5 to 4 L) slow cooker. Scatter bacon over turkey.

Add remaining 3 ingredients, 2 cups (500 mL) water and a sprinkle of pepper to same frying pan. Heat and stir, scraping any brown bits from bottom of pan, until boiling. Add to slow cooker. Stir. Cook, covered, on Low for 6 to 7 hours or on High for 3 to 3 1/2 hours until rice is tender. Makes about 6 cups (1.5 L).

1 cup (250 mL): 186 Calories; 6.7 g Total Fat (1.7 g Mono, 0.7 g Poly, 2.0 g Sat); 7 mg Cholesterol; 26 g Carbohydrate; 2 g Fibre; 6 g Protein; 664 mg Sodium

Orange Chicken and Rice

Vibrant citrus flavour infuses light and fluffy rice, served alongside tender, seasoned chicken.

Medium oranges	2	2
Long-grain white rice	2 cups	500 mL
Prepared chicken broth	2 cups	500 mL
Italian dressing, divided	1/3 cup	75 mL
Boneless, skinless chicken thighs	1 1/2 lbs.	680 g

Grate 1 tsp. (5 mL) orange zest into 3 1/2 to 4 quart (3.5 to 4 L) slow cooker. Squeeze 1/2 cup (125 mL) orange juice and pour into slow cooker.

Add rice, broth, 2 tbsp. (30 mL) dressing, 1 cup (250 mL) water and a generous sprinkle of salt and pepper. Stir.

Put chicken into medium bowl. Sprinkle with salt. Pour remaining dressing over top. Stir until coated. Heat large greased frying pan on medium-high. Add chicken. Discard any remaining dressing. Cook for about 3 minutes per side until browned. Arrange over rice mixture. Cook, covered, on Low for 4 to 5 hours or High for 2 to 2 1/2 hours. Serves 6.

1 serving: 466 Calories; 13.8 g Total Fat (4.0 g Mono, 2.4 g Poly, 3.1 g Sat); 74 mg Cholesterol; 56 g Carbohydrate; 1 g Fibre; 26 g Protein; 1012 mg Sodium

Sweet Chili Chicken

Tender, sweet chicken with a hint of chili will be a hit with the kids! Make it a meal with rice and steamed vegetables.

Boneless, skinless chicken thighs	2 lbs.	900 g
Prepared chicken broth	2/3 cup	150 mL
Sweet chili sauce	1/2 cup	125 mL
Minute tapioca	3 tbsp.	50 mL
Soy sauce	1 tbsp.	15 mL

Heat large greased frying pan on medium-high. Add chicken. Sprinkle with salt and pepper. Cook for about 3 minutes per side until browned. Transfer to 3 1/2 to 4 quart (3.5 to 4 L) slow cooker.

(continued on next page)

Combine broth, 1/4 cup (60 mL) chili sauce, tapioca and soy sauce in small bowl. Pour over chicken. Cook, covered, on Low for 6 to 7 hours or on High for 3 to 3 1/2 hours. Add remaining chili sauce. Stir. Serves 8.

1 serving: 213 Calories; 9.2 g Total Fat (3.6 g Mono, 2.1 g Poly, 2.4 g Sat); 74 mg Cholesterol; 10 g Carbohydrate; trace Fibre; 21 g Protein; 571 mg Sodium

Cranberry Chicken Wings

These tasty wings are glazed with sweet and savoury sauce with a hint of cranberry tartness.

Split chicken wings, tips discarded	3 lbs.	1.4 kg
Can of jellied cranberry sauce	14 oz.	398 mL
Barbecue sauce	1/2 cup	125 mL
Brown sugar, packed	1/4 cup	60 mL
Dijon mustard	2 tsp.	10 mL

Arrange chicken wings on greased baking sheet with sides. Broil on top rack in oven for about 6 minutes per side until browned. Transfer to 3 1/2 to 4 quart (3.5 to 4 L) slow cooker.

Whisk remaining 4 ingredients in medium bowl until smooth. Pour over chicken. Cook, covered, on Low for 4 to 5 hours or on High for 2 to 2 1/2 hours, stirring at halftime. Makes about 36 pieces.

1 piece: 109 Calories; 6.1 g Total Fat (trace Mono, trace Poly, 1.6 g Sat); 28 mg Cholesterol; 6 g Carbohydrate; trace Fibre; 7 g Protein; 63 mg Sodium

Paré Pointer

You know a cat burglar has been in your house if your cat is missing.

Turkey Goulash

A hearty goulash, rich with flavourful turkey and paprika. Serve over egg noodles or spaetzle and garnish with a dollop of sour cream and a sprinkle of chopped fresh dill.

Can of tomato paste	5 1/2 oz.	156 mL
Minute tapioca	3 tbsp.	50 mL
Envelope of onion soup mix	1 1/2 oz.	42 g
Paprika	1 tbsp.	15 mL
Boneless, skinless turkey thighs, cut into 3/4 inch (2 cm) pieces	2 lbs.	900 g

Combine first 4 ingredients, 2 1/2 cups (625 mL) water and a sprinkle of salt and pepper in 4 to 5 quart (4 to 5 L) slow cooker.

Add turkey. Stir. Cook, covered, on Low for 6 to 7 hours or on High for 3 to 3 1/2 hours. Makes about 7 cups (1.75 L).

3/4 cup (175 mL): 163 Calories; 4.5 g Total Fat (1.1 g Mono, 1.3 g Poly, 1.5 g Sat); 66 mg Cholesterol; 10 g Carbohydrate; 1 g Fibre; 2 g Protein; 554 mg Sodium

Cajun Turkey Stew

Tender turkey and potatoes in a spicy tomato sauce—with okra for Southern authenticity. Corn or lima beans can be substituted if you prefer.

Boneless, skinless turkey thighs, cut into 1 1/2 inch (3.8 cm) pieces	2 lbs.	900 g
Cajun seasoning, divided	3 tbsp.	50 mL
Red baby potatoes, quartered	2 lbs.	900 g
Can of diced tomatoes (with juice)	28 oz.	796 mL
Chopped fresh (or frozen, thawed) okra	2 cups	500 mL

Put turkey into medium bowl. Sprinkle with 1 tbsp. (15 mL) Cajun seasoning. Stir until coated. Heat large greased frying pan on medium-high. Cook turkey, in 2 batches, for about 5 minutes, stirring occasionally, until browned. Transfer to 4 to 5 quart (4 to 5 L) slow cooker. Add 1/2 cup (125 mL) water to same frying pan. Heat and stir, scraping any brown bits from bottom of pan, until boiling. Add to slow cooker.

(continued on next page)

Add remaining 3 ingredients and 1 tbsp. (15 mL) Cajun seasoning. Stir. Cook, covered, on Low for 8 to 10 hours or on High for 4 to 5 hours. Add remaining Cajun seasoning. Stir. Makes about 10 cups (2.5 L).

1 cup (250 mL): 211 Calories; 4.5 g Total Fat (1.2 g Mono, 1.3 g Poly, 1.4 g Sat); 63 mg Cholesterol; 21 g Carbohydrate; 2 g Fibre; 21 g Protein; 779 mg Sodium

Pictured on page 72.

Shiitake Ginger Chicken

This sweet and spicy sauce infuses chicken morsels and shiitake mushrooms with wonderful ginger flavour.

Thinly sliced fresh shiitake mushrooms	2 cups	500 mL
Boneless, skinless chicken thighs	2 lbs.	900 g
Ginger marmalade	3/4 cup	175 mL
Soy sauce	3 tbsp.	50 mL
Finely grated ginger root	2 tbsp.	30 mL

Heat large greased frying pan on medium. Add mushrooms. Cook for about 5 minutes, stirring often, until mushrooms start to release their liquid. Transfer to 3 1/2 to 4 quart (3.5 to 4 L) slow cooker.

Arrange chicken over mushrooms.

Combine remaining 3 ingredients and 1/3 cup (75 mL) water in small bowl. Pour over chicken. Cook, covered, on Low for 5 to 6 hours or on High for 2 1/2 to 3 hours. Transfer chicken and half of solids with slotted spoon to large serving platter. Cover to keep warm. Skim and discard fat from cooking liquid. Carefully process with remaining solids in blender until smooth (see Safety Tip). Pour sauce over chicken and mushrooms. Serves 8.

1 serving: 254 Calories; 9.2 g Total Fat (3.6 g Mono, 2.1 g Poly, 2.4 g Sat); 74 mg Cholesterol; 22 g Carbohydrate; 1 g Fibre; 22 g Protein; 582 mg Sodium

Safety Tip: Follow manufacturer's instructions for processing hot liquids.

Thai Green Curry Chicken

This saucy curry has melt-in-your-mouth chicken, crisp colourful vegetables and an authentic coconut flavour. Serve with fragrant jasmine or basmati rice.

Boneless, skinless chicken thighs, halved	2 lbs.	900 g
Thai green curry paste	2 tbsp.	30 mL
Can of coconut milk	14 oz.	398 mL
Cornstarch	2 tbsp.	30 mL
Frozen Oriental mixed vegetables, thawed	4 1/2 cups	1.1 L

Heat large well-greased frying pan on medium-high. Cook chicken, in 2 batches, for about 3 minutes per side until browned. Transfer to 4 to 5 quart (4 to 5 L) slow cooker. Sprinkle with salt and pepper.

Add curry paste and 1 1/2 cups (375 mL) water to same frying pan. Heat and stir, scraping any brown bits from bottom of pan, until boiling. Add to slow cooker. Cook, covered, on Low for 6 to 7 hours or on High for 3 to 3 1/2 hours.

Stir coconut milk into cornstarch in medium bowl until smooth. Add to chicken mixture. Stir. Add vegetables. Stir. Cook, covered, on High for about 45 minutes until bubbling. Makes about 7 1/2 cups (1.9 L).

1 cup (250 mL): 337 Calories; 23.1 g Total Fat (5.0 g Mono, 2.7 g Poly, 12.9 g Sat); 79 mg Cholesterol; 9 g Carbohydrate; 2 g Fibre; 24 g Protein; 326 mg Sodium

1. Toffee Pudding Cake, page 140
2. Tri-Colour Turkey Roll, page 80

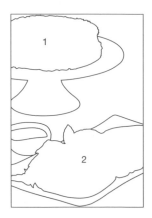

Chicken Stew

For a family-friendly meal, nothing beats a simple yet hearty chicken stew with rich, comforting flavours and don't forget biscuits for dipping!

Halved red (or yellow) baby potatoes	2 cups	500 mL
Boneless, skinless chicken thighs, cut into 1 inch (2.5 cm) pieces	1 1/2 lbs.	680 g
Poultry seasoning	1/2 tsp.	2 mL
Envelopes of chicken gravy mix (1 oz., 31 g, each)	2	2
Frozen pea and carrot mix, thawed	2 cups	500 mL

Put potatoes into 3 1/2 to 4 quart (3.5 to 4 L) slow cooker. Arrange chicken over top. Sprinkle with poultry seasoning, salt and pepper.

Combine gravy mix and 2 cups (500 mL) water in medium bowl. Pour over chicken. Cook, covered, on Low for 6 to 8 hours or on High for 3 to 4 hours.

Add peas and carrots. Stir. Cook, covered, on High for about 30 minutes until vegetables are tender. Makes about 8 cups (2 L).

1 cup (250 mL): 207 Calories; 7.6 g Total Fat (2.4 g Mono, 1.5 g Poly, 1.8 g Sat); 56 mg Cholesterol; 16 g Carbohydrate; 2 g Fibre; 17 g Protein; 498 mg Sodium

Pictured on page 72.

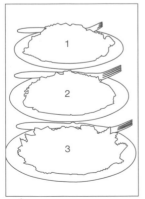

1. Italiano Pasta Sauce, page 97
2. Veggie Pasta Sauce, page 129
3. Chicken Sausage Pasta Sauce, page 92

Chicken and Rice Casserole

When you're in need of comfort food, settle in with a bowl of this creamy rice casserole full of broccoli and tender chicken pieces.

Long-grain brown rice	1 1/2 cups	375 mL
Can of condensed cream of broccoli soup	10 oz.	284 mL
Can of condensed cream of chicken soup	10 oz.	284 mL
Boneless, skinless chicken thighs	1 1/2 lbs.	680 g
Frozen chopped broccoli, thawed	3 cups	750 mL

Combine first 3 ingredients and 1 1/2 cups (375 mL) water in greased 3 1/2 to 4 quart (3.5 to 4 L) slow cooker.

Heat large greased frying pan on medium-high. Add chicken. Sprinkle with salt and pepper. Cook for about 3 minutes per side until browned. Arrange chicken over rice mixture in slow cooker. Cook, covered, on Low for 6 to 7 hours or on High for 3 to 3 1/2 hours.

Add broccoli. Stir. Cook, covered, on High for about 15 minutes until broccoli is tender. Makes about 7 1/2 cups (1.9 L).

1 cup (250 mL): 368 Calories; 12.3 g Total Fat (4.0 g Mono, 2.9 g Poly, 3.1 g Sat); 64 mg Cholesterol; 41 g Carbohydrate; 5 g Fibre; 24 g Protein; 687 mg Sodium

Chicken Sausage Pasta Sauce

A thick and chunky pasta sauce that's best served with bite-sized pastas. This can also be used in your favourite lasagna recipe.

Chicken (or turkey) sausage, casing removed	1 1/2 lbs.	680 g
Finely chopped onion	1/2 cup	125 mL
Tomato basil pasta sauce	3 cups	750 mL
Chopped fresh white mushrooms	1 cup	250 mL
Chopped zucchini (with peel)	1 cup	250 mL

Scramble-fry sausage and onion in large greased frying pan on medium-high for about 10 minutes, until sausage is no longer pink. Drain. Transfer to 4 to 5 quart (4 to 5 L) slow cooker.

(continued on next page)

Add remaining 3 ingredients. Stir. Cook, covered, on Low for 4 to 5 hours or on High for 2 to 2 1/2 hours. Makes about 6 cups (1.5 L).

1/2 cup (125 mL): 149 Calories; 7.5 g Total Fat (1.7 g Mono, 0.9 g Poly, 3.6 g Sat); 40 mg Cholesterol; 6 g Carbohydrate; trace Fibre; 13 g Protein; 277 mg Sodium

Pictured on page 90.

Satay Chicken Stew

The flavours of peanut butter and tomato are a tasty combo in this mildly spicy chicken stew—great served over rice or mashed sweet potatoes.

Boneless, skinless chicken breast halves, cut into 1 inch (2.5 cm) cubes	1 1/2 lbs.	680 g
Quartered fresh white mushrooms	3 cups	750 mL
Hot salsa	1 1/2 cups	375 mL
Tomato paste	2 tbsp.	30 mL
Crunchy peanut butter	1/2 cup	125 mL

Heat large greased frying pan on medium-high. Add chicken. Sprinkle with pepper. Cook for about 6 minutes, stirring occasionally, until browned. Transfer to 3 1/2 to 4 quart (3.5 to 4 L) slow cooker.

Add mushrooms to same greased frying pan. Cook for about 5 minutes, stirring occasionally, until starting to brown. Add to slow cooker.

Combine salsa, tomato paste and 1/2 cup (125 mL) water in small bowl. Pour over mushrooms. Cook, covered, on Low for 6 to 7 hours or on High for 3 to 3 1/2 hours.

Add peanut butter. Stir well. Makes about 4 cups (1 L).

3/4 cup (175 mL): 349 Calories; 17.8 g Total Fat (2.4 g Mono, 1.4 g Poly, 3.5 g Sat); 75 mg Cholesterol; 13 g Carbohydrate; 2 g Fibre; 34 g Protein; 431 mg Sodium

Chicken in Mushroom Sauce

Creamy, smoky bacon and mushroom sauce coats well-seasoned chicken, perfect to serve over a bed of noodles.

Bacon slices, diced	6	6
Boneless, skinless chicken thighs	2 lbs.	900 g
Can of condensed cream of mushroom and onion soup	10 oz.	284 mL
Prepared chicken broth	1 cup	250 mL
Dried thyme	3/4 tsp.	4 mL

Cook bacon in large frying pan on medium until crisp. Transfer with slotted spoon to paper towel-lined plate to drain. Drain and discard all but 1 tbsp. (15 mL) drippings.

Cook chicken in same frying pan, in 2 batches, for about 5 minutes per side until browned. Transfer with slotted spoon to 3 1/2 to 4 quart (3.5 to 4 L) slow cooker. Drain and discard drippings. Scatter bacon over chicken. Sprinkle with pepper.

Add remaining 3 ingredients and 1 cup (250 mL) water to same frying pan. Heat and stir, scraping any brown bits from bottom of pan, until boiling. Add to slow cooker. Cook, covered, on Low for 6 to 7 hours or on High for 3 to 3 1/2 hours. Serves 8.

1 serving: 236 Calories; 14.3 g Total Fat (4.9 g Mono, 2.4 g Poly, 4.1 g Sat); 83 mg Cholesterol; 3 g Carbohydrate; trace Fibre; 23 g Protein; 619 mg Sodium

Paré Pointer

He promised her the world at her feet, but what she really wanted was a roof over their heads.

Lemonade Chicken

What says summer better than lemonade and barbecued chicken? Combine them in this flavourful chicken-and-potato meal and recreate the taste of summer all year round.

All-purpose flour	1/3 cup	75 mL
Bone-in chicken thighs, skin removed	3 lbs.	1.4 kg
Baby potatoes, larger ones cut in half	1 lb.	454 g
Frozen concentrated lemonade, thawed	3/4 cup	175 mL
Barbecue sauce	1/4 cup	60 mL

Combine flour and a sprinkle of salt and pepper in large resealable freezer bag. Add chicken. Seal bag. Toss until coated. Remove chicken. Discard any remaining flour mixture.

Put potatoes into 3 1/2 to 4 quart (3.5 to 4 L) slow cooker. Arrange chicken over top.

Combine concentrated lemonade and barbecue sauce in small bowl. Pour over chicken. Cook, covered, on Low for 8 to 10 hours or on High for 4 to 5 hours. Serves 4.

1 serving: 607 Calories; 20.1 g Total Fat (7.6 g Mono, 4.6 g Poly, 5.5 g Sat); 172 mg Cholesterol; 53 g Carbohydrate; 2 g Fibre; 51 g Protein; 441 mg Sodium

Sweet-and-Sour Pork Chops

Pork and pineapple pair up in a sweet, tangy and lemony sauce—another great dish to serve alongside lots of fluffy rice.

Boneless pork shoulder butt steaks, trimmed of fat, cut in half	3 lbs.	1.4 kg
Can of crushed pineapple (with juice)	14 oz.	398 mL
Lemon pie filling powder (not instant), stir before measuring	9 tbsp.	150 mL
Ketchup	1/2 cup	125 mL
Medium lemon	1	1

Heat large well-greased frying pan on medium-high. Add half of pork. Sprinkle generously with salt and pepper. Cook pork for 2 to 3 minutes per side until browned. Repeat with remaining pork. Transfer to 4 to 5 quart (4 to 5 L) slow cooker.

Combine next 3 ingredients in medium bowl.

Grate 1/2 tsp. (2 mL) lemon zest into small bowl. Set aside. Squeeze 2 tbsp. (30 mL) lemon juice into pineapple mixture. Stir. Pour over pork. Cook, covered, on Low for 6 to 7 hours or on High for 3 to 3 1/2 hours. Add lemon zest. Stir. Serves 8.

1 serving: 390 Calories; 16.9 g Total Fat (7.5 g Mono, 1.5 g Poly, 6.2 g Sat); 101 mg Cholesterol; 29 g Carbohydrate; trace Fibre; 31 g Protein; 306 mg Sodium

Bratwurst Stew

Sausage makes a unique substitute for beef in this stew, and adds richness to the sauce. A filling and hearty meal!

Baby potatoes, larger ones cut in half	2 lbs.	900 g
Baby carrots	3 cups	750 mL
Uncooked bratwurst sausage, cut into 2 inch (5 cm) pieces	2 lbs.	900 g
Can of condensed onion soup	10 oz.	284 mL
Sour cream	1/4 cup	60 mL

(continued on next page)

Layer first 3 ingredients, in order given, in 4 to 5 quart (4 to 5 L) slow cooker. Sprinkle generously with pepper.

Pour soup over top. Cook, covered, on Low for 8 to 10 hours or on High for 4 to 5 hours. Transfer sausage, potato and carrot with slotted spoon to large serving platter. Cover to keep warm. Skim and discard fat from cooking liquid.

Add sour cream. Stir until combined. Pour sauce over sausage and vegetables. Serves 8.

1 serving: 482 Calories; 31.6 g Total Fat (9.3 g Mono, 2.0 g Poly, 7.8 g Sat); 93 mg Cholesterol; 29 g Carbohydrate; 3 g Fibre; 18 g Protein; 1443 mg Sodium

Italiano Pasta Sauce

Serve this sweet tomato sauce over your favourite pasta for a delicious meal anytime! Sausage, onion and artichoke add richness and hearty textures.

Cans of Italian-style stewed tomatoes (19 oz., 540 g, each), cut up	2	2
Hot Italian sausage, casing removed	1 lb.	454 g
Chopped onion	1 cup	250 mL
Cans of artichoke hearts (14 oz., 398 mL, each), drained, quartered	2	2
Tomato basil pasta sauce	4 cups	1 L

Put tomatoes into 4 to 5 quart (4 to 5 L) slow cooker.

Scramble-fry sausage and onion in large greased frying pan on medium-high for about 8 minutes until sausage is no longer pink. Drain. Add to slow cooker.

Add artichoke and pasta sauce. Stir. Cook, covered, on Low for 6 to 8 hours or on High for 3 to 4 hours. Makes about 12 cups (3 L).

3/4 cup (175 mL): 182 Calories; 9.3 g Total Fat (3.6 g Mono, 1.0 g Poly, 2.7 g Sat); 16 mg Cholesterol; 14 g Carbohydrate; 1 g Fibre; 9 g Protein; 849 mg Sodium

Pictured on page 90.

Country Ribs and Sauerkraut

This simple dish adds tomatoes to the classic combination of pork ribs, onion and sauerkraut—the result is a blend of savoury, sweet and sour flavours, and a dish that feeds a crowd!

Can of diced tomatoes, drained	19 oz.	540 mL
Can of wine sauerkraut, rinsed and drained	14 oz.	398 mL
Chopped onion	1 cup	250 mL
Brown sugar, packed	1/2 cup	125 mL
Boneless country-style pork ribs	3 lbs.	1.4 kg

Combine first 4 ingredients in large bowl. Transfer half of sauerkraut mixture to 3 1/2 to 4 quart (3.5 to 4 L) slow cooker.

Add ribs. Spoon remaining sauerkraut mixture over ribs. Cook, covered, on Low for 8 to 9 hours or on High for 4 to 4 1/2 hours. Makes about 8 cups (2 L).

1 cup (250 mL): 457 Calories; 27.4 g Total Fat (11.8 g Mono, 2.5 g Poly, 10.2 g Sat); 111 mg Cholesterol; 20 g Carbohydrate; 2 g Fibre; 31 g Protein; 563 mg Sodium

Irish Stew

There's an extra touch of "Irish" brewed into this simple lamb and vegetable stew—dark stout beer, such as Ireland's famous Guinness, is simmered in the broth.

Baby potatoes, larger ones cut in half	1 lb.	454 g
Baby carrots	2 cups	500 mL
Boneless lamb shoulder, trimmed of fat and cut into 1 1/2 inch (3.8 cm) pieces	3 lbs.	1.4 kg
Stout beer	1 3/4 cups	425 mL
Can of condensed onion soup	10 oz.	284 mL

Combine potatoes and carrot in 5 to 7 quart (5 to 7 L) slow cooker.

Sprinkle lamb with salt and pepper. Heat large well-greased frying pan on medium-high. Cook lamb, in 2 batches, for about 5 minutes, stirring occasionally, until browned. Add to slow cooker.

(continued on next page)

Add beer and soup to same frying pan. Heat and stir, scraping any brown bits from bottom of pan, until boiling. Add to slow cooker. Stir. Cook, covered, on Low for 8 to 10 hours or on High for 4 to 5 hours. Makes about 9 cups (2.25 L).

1 cup (250 mL): 417 Calories; 23.3 g Total Fat (9.3 g Mono, 2.1 g Poly, 9.2 g Sat); 111 mg Cholesterol; 16 g Carbohydrate; 1 g Fibre; 30 g Protein; 397 mg Sodium

Pictured on page 107.

Variation: You can substitute a honey brown or a lager beer if you want a lighter tasting broth.

Greek Pasta Bake

This filling dish features tomato-saucy pasta with lots of lemony ground lamb for a Greek flair. Round it out with a Greek salad and garlic toast.

Lean ground lamb	1 1/2 lbs.	680 g
Greek seasoning	1 tbsp.	15 mL
Grated lemon zest	1 tsp.	5 mL
Four-cheese tomato pasta sauce	4 cups	1 L
Cooked rigatoni pasta (about 3 cups, 750 mL, uncooked)	5 cups	1.25 L

Scramble-fry lamb in large greased frying pan on medium-high for about 10 minutes until no longer pink.

Add Greek seasoning, lemon zest and a sprinkle of salt and pepper. Stir.

To assemble, layer ingredients in greased 5 to 7 quart (5 to 7 L) slow cooker as follows:

1. 3/4 cup (175 mL) pasta sauce
2. 1/3 of pasta
3. 1 cup (250 mL) lamb mixture

Repeat steps 1 to 3 to make 2 more layers. Top with remaining pasta sauce.

Cook, covered, on Low for 3 to 4 hours or on High for 1 1/2 to 2 hours until heated through. Serves 8.

1 serving: 450 Calories; 20.7 g Total Fat (7.4 g Mono, 1.4 g Poly, 7.0 g Sat); 83 mg Cholesterol; 37 g Carbohydrate; 3 g Fibre; 27 g Protein; 792 mg Sodium

Sausage Cabbage Stew

This hearty stew has a colourful mix of meat and vegetables and a peppery kick to keep you cozy on a cold winter's day.

Hot Italian sausage, casing removed	1 1/2 lbs.	680 g
Chopped onion	1 1/2 cups	375 mL
Diced peeled potato	3 cups	750 mL
Cans of stewed tomatoes	2	2
(14 oz., 398 mL, each)		
Shredded cabbage	4 cups	1 L

Scramble-fry sausage and onion in large greased frying pan on medium-high for about 12 minutes until sausage is no longer pink. Drain. Transfer to 3 1/2 to 4 quart (3.5 to 4 L) slow cooker.

Add potato, tomatoes, 1 cup (250 mL) of water and a sprinkle of salt and pepper. Stir. Cook, covered, on Low for 6 to 7 hours or on High for 3 to 3 1/2 hours.

Add cabbage. Stir. Cook, covered, on High for about 1 hour until cabbage is tender. Makes about 8 3/4 cups (2.2 L).

1 cup (250 mL): 379 Calories; 21.9 g Total Fat (9.6 g Mono, 2.8 g Poly, 7.5 g Sat); 44 mg Cholesterol; 28 g Carbohydrate; 3 g Fibre; 18 g Protein; 1404 mg Sodium

Sweet-and-Sour Pork Ribs

The classic flavours of sweet and sour are infused into these delicious pork ribs. Serve with white rice for a crowd-pleasing meal.

Pork side ribs, trimmed of fat and cut into 3-bone portions	3 lbs.	1.4 kg
Rice vinegar	2 tbsp.	30 mL
Garlic cloves, minced (or 1/2 tsp., 2 mL, powder)	2	2
Grated ginger root (or 1/2 tsp., 2 mL, powder)	2 tsp.	10 mL
Sweet-and-sour sauce	3 cups	750 mL

(continued on next page)

Heat large greased frying pan on medium-high. Add ribs. Sprinkle with salt and pepper. Cook for about 2 minutes per side until browned. Transfer to 3 1/2 to 4 quart (3.5 to 4 L) slow cooker.

Combine next 3 ingredients and 2 cups (500 mL) sweet-and-sour sauce in medium bowl. Pour over ribs. Cook, covered, on Low for 8 to 9 hours or on High for 4 to 4 1/2 hours. Transfer ribs to large shallow bowl. Cover to keep warm. Skim and discard fat from cooking liquid. Add remaining sweet-and-sour sauce. Stir. Pour over ribs. Makes ten 3-bone portions.

1 portion: 605 Calories; 43.1 g Total Fat (18.6 g Mono, 3.3 g Poly, 15.0 g Sat); 161 mg Cholesterol; 20 g Carbohydrate; trace Fibre; 33 g Protein; 472 mg Sodium

Hoisin Honey Ribs

These sweet, saucy and very tender pork ribs have an Asian flavour that goes well with basmati rice and stir-fry vegetables.

Hoisin sauce	1/2 cup	125 mL
Liquid honey	1/2 cup	125 mL
Soy sauce	1/3 cup	75 mL
Garlic cloves, minced (or 1/2 tsp., 2 mL, powder)	2	2
Pork side ribs, trimmed of fat and cut into 3-bone portions	3 lbs.	1.4 kg

Combine first 4 ingredients in large bowl. Reserve 1/3 cup (75 mL).

Add ribs. Stir until coated. Transfer to 3 1/2 to 4 quart (3.5 to 4 L) slow cooker. Cook, covered, on Low for 8 to 9 hours or on High for 4 to 4 1/2 hours. Transfer ribs to serving platter. Brush with reserved hoisin mixture. Makes ten 3-bone portions.

1 portion: 558 Calories; 40.3 g Total Fat (18.3 Mono, 3.2 g Poly, 15.0 g Sat); 161 mg Cholesterol; 22 g Carbohydrate; trace Fibre; 34 g Protein; 1270 mg Sodium

Braised Pork Steaks

These fork-tender pork steaks are a Southern-style treat! The thick, tasty sauce coats the steaks well, and would be perfect to serve with mashed potatoes and a side of warm biscuits.

All-purpose flour	1/2 cup	125 mL
Montreal steak spice	1 tbsp.	15 mL
Boneless pork shoulder blade steaks, cut in half	1 1/2 lbs.	680 g
Prepared chicken broth	1 cup	250 mL
Dijon mustard	2 tbsp.	30 mL

Combine flour and steak spice in large resealable freezer bag. Add pork. Turn to coat. Heat large well-greased frying pan on medium-high. Add pork. Reserve remaining flour mixture. Cook for 2 to 3 minutes per side until browned. Transfer to 4 to 5 quart (4 to 5 L) slow cooker.

Add reserved flour mixture to same frying pan. Heat and stir for 1 minute. Gradually add broth and 1 1/2 cups (375 mL) water, whisking constantly until smooth. Heat and stir for 1 to 2 minutes until starting to thicken. Pour over pork. Cook, covered, on Low for 6 to 7 hours or on High for 3 to 3 1/2 hours. Transfer pork with slotted spoon to serving platter.

Add mustard to sauce. Stir. Makes about 1 1/2 cups (375 mL) sauce. Serve with pork. Serves 6.

1 serving with 1/4 cup (60 mL) sauce: 240 Calories; 13.8 g Total Fat (6.4 g Mono, 1.8 g Poly, 4.3 g Sat); 67 mg Cholesterol; 8 g Carbohydrate; trace Fibre; 20 g Protein; 682 mg Sodium

Barbecued Pulled Pork

If you've got a crowd to feed, serve up a batch of this tangy pulled pork with split hamburger or Kaiser buns. Try serving this Memphis-style, with a few spoonfuls of well-drained coleslaw right in your bun.

Boneless pork shoulder butt roasts (about 2 3/4 lbs., 1.25 kg, each)	2	2
Hickory barbecue sauce	3 cups	750 mL
Apple cider vinegar	3 tbsp.	50 mL
Garlic cloves, minced (or 1 tsp., 5 mL, powder)	4	4
Worcestershire sauce	2 tsp.	10 mL

Put roasts into 5 to 7 quart (5 to 7 L) slow cooker.

Combine 2 cups barbecue sauce, remaining 3 ingredients and 1/2 cup (125 mL) water in medium bowl. Pour over roasts. Cook, covered, on High for 4 to 5 hours until tender. Transfer roasts to large plate. Shred pork using 2 forks. Remove and discard any visible fat. Skim and discard fat from sauce. Return pork to sauce. Add remaining barbecue sauce. Stir. Cook, covered, on High for 30 minutes until heated through. Makes about 10 cups (2.5 L).

1/2 cup (125 mL): 375 Calories; 17.9 g Total Fat (7.9 g Mono, 1.6 g Poly, 6.5 g Sat); 106 mg Cholesterol; 21 g Carbohydrate; trace Fibre; 30 g Protein; 417 mg Sodium

Pictured on page 54.

Paré Pointer

Of course you know that a policeman's uniform is really a lawsuit.

Cabbage Pork Dinner

This delicious, all-in-one dinner is ready to eat when you walk in the door. Garnish with fresh dill for a fabulous finish to this easy meal.

Baby potatoes, larger ones cut in half	1 1/2 lbs.	680 g
Coleslaw mix, lightly packed	7 cups	1.75 L
Boneless pork shoulder blade steak, cut into 1 inch (2.5 cm) pieces	1 1/2 lbs.	680 g
Chopped onion	1 cup	250 mL
Tomato cream pasta sauce	2 2/3 cups	650 mL

Put potatoes into greased 4 to 5 quart (4 to 5 L) slow cooker. Spread coleslaw mix evenly over top. Sprinkle with salt and pepper.

Heat large greased frying pan on medium-high. Add pork. Sprinkle with pepper. Cook for about 5 minutes, stirring occasionally, until browned. Arrange over cabbage.

Add onion to same greased frying pan. Reduce heat to medium. Cook for about 5 minutes, stirring often, until softened. Spread evenly over pork.

Pour pasta sauce over onion. Do not stir. Cook, covered, on Low for 5 to 6 hours or on High for 2 1/2 to 3 hours. Makes about 8 cups (2 L).

1 cup (250 mL): 270 Calories; 10.4 g Total Fat (4.4 g Mono, 1.1 g Poly, 3.2 g Sat); 50 mg Cholesterol; 26 g Carbohydrate; 3 g Fibre; 19 g Protein; 358 mg Sodium

Herb Dijon Roast Lamb

This tender roast lamb has lots of delicious herb and mustard flavours—try thickening the cooking liquid into a rich gravy to serve with lemony Greek potatoes and fresh vegetables.

Dijon mustard (with whole seeds)	1/4 cup	60 mL
Dried thyme	1 tsp.	5 mL
Dried rosemary, crushed	1/2 tsp.	2 mL
Garlic clove, minced (or 1/4 tsp., 1 mL, powder)	1	1
Centre cut leg of lamb	4 lbs.	1.8 kg

(continued on next page)

Put an even layer (2 to 3 inches, 5 to 7.5 cm, thick) of crumpled foil into bottom of 7 quart (7 L) slow cooker (see Tip, page 80). Combine first 4 ingredients and a sprinkle of salt and pepper in small bowl. Brush over roast. Place roast, fat-side up, onto foil in slow cooker. Cook, covered, on High for 4 to 5 hours. Transfer roast to cutting board. Cover with foil. Let stand for 10 minutes. Carefully remove and discard foil from slow cooker. Skim and discard fat from cooking liquid. Makes about 1 1/2 cups (375 mL) cooking liquid. Cut roast into thin slices. Serve with cooking liquid. Serves 10.

1 serving with 2 1/2 tbsp (37 mL) cooking liquid: 426 Calories; 31.5 g Total Fat (12.7 g Mono, 2.5 g Poly, 13.5 g Sat); 125 mg Cholesterol; 1 g Carbohydrate; trace Fibre; 33 g Protein; 283 mg Sodium

---

Chili Rhubarb Pork

This lean and moist pork roast has a sweet fruity sauce with a hint of spicy heat—just the thing to jazz up your next Sunday dinner.

Boneless pork loin roast	3 lbs.	1.4 kg
Frozen rhubarb, thawed	1 cup	250 mL
Ketchup	1/2 cup	125 mL
Brown sugar, packed	1/4 cup	60 mL
Chili paste (sambal oelek)	2 tsp.	10 mL

Sprinkle roast with salt and pepper. Cook in large greased frying pan on medium-high for about 8 minutes, turning occasionally, until browned on all sides. Transfer to 4 to 5 quart (4 to 5 L) slow cooker.

Process remaining 4 ingredients and 1 cup (250 mL) water in blender or food processor until smooth. Pour over roast. Cook, covered, on Low for 8 to 9 hours or on High for 4 to 4 1/2 hours. Transfer roast to cutting board. Cover with foil. Let stand for 10 minutes. Skim and discard fat from cooking liquid. Carefully process liquid in blender until smooth (see Safety Tip). Makes about 2 1/2 cups (625 mL) sauce. Cut roast into thin slices. Serve with sauce. Serves 10.

1 serving 1/4 cup (60 mL) sauce: 332 Calories; 13.6 g Total Fat (6.2 g Mono, 1.2 g Poly, 4.8 g Sat); 110 mg Cholesterol; 12 g Carbohydrate; trace Fibre; 39 g Protein; 249 mg Sodium

Safety Tip: Follow manufacturer's instructions for processing hot liquids.

Mango Chutney Pork

Tender pork medallions and a sweet, tangy chutney sauce would look lovely dished up over a bowl of fluffy rice.

Mango chutney	3/4 cup	175 mL
Hot curry paste	2 tbsp.	30 mL
Thinly sliced onion	2 cups	500 mL
Pork tenderloin, trimmed of fat and cut into 1/2 inch (12 mm) slices	2 lbs.	900 g
Chopped red pepper	1 1/2 cups	375 mL

Process chutney, curry paste and 2/3 cup (150 mL) water in blender or food processor until smooth.

Heat large greased frying pan on medium. Add onion. Cook for about 10 minutes, stirring often, until softened. Transfer to 3 1/2 to 4 quart (3.5 to 4 L) slow cooker.

Increase heat to medium-high Add half of pork to same greased frying pan. Sprinkle with salt and pepper. Cook for about 2 minutes per side until browned. Arrange over onion. Repeat with remaining pork.

Scatter red pepper over pork. Pour curry mixture over top. Do not stir. Cook, covered, on Low for 6 to 8 hours or on High for 3 to 4 hours. Makes about 4 cups (1 L).

1/2 cup (125 mL): 236 Calories; 8.2 g Total Fat (2.4 g Mono, 0.8 g Poly, 1.7 g Sat); 74 mg Cholesterol; 16 g Carbohydrate; 1 g Fibre; 24 g Protein; 493 mg Sodium

Pictured at right.

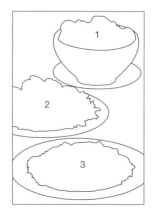

1. Irish Stew, page 98
2. Mushroom Pork Marsala, page 111
3. Mango Chutney Pork, above

French Lamb Casserole

This rich, comforting dish was inspired by the classic French cassoulet (ka-soo-LAY). Make it a meal with a fresh baguette, steamed green beans and a bottle of wine.

Lamb shank, trimmed of fat, meat cut into 3/4 inch (2 cm) pieces, bone reserved (see Note)	1 lb.	454 g
Can of diced tomatoes (with juice)	28 oz.	796 mL
Cans of black-eyed peas (19 oz., 540 mL each), rinsed and drained	2	2
Smoked ham sausage, cut into 1/4 inch (6 mm) slices	4 oz.	113 g
Onion soup mix, stir before measuring	3 tbsp.	50 mL

Heat medium greased frying pan on medium-high. Add lamb. Cook for about 8 minutes, stirring occasionally, until browned. Transfer to 4 to 5 quart (4 to 5 L) slow cooker.

Add remaining 4 ingredients and reserved bone. Stir. Cook, covered, on Low for 8 to 10 hours or on High for 4 to 5 hours. Remove and discard bone. Makes about 6 cups (1.5 L).

1 cup (250 mL): 276 Calories; 10.1 g Total Fat (2.1 g Mono, 0.5 g Poly, 3.5 g Sat); 39 mg Cholesterol; 32 g Carbohydrate; 6 g Fibre; 20 g Protein; 2017 mg Sodium

Pictured at left.

Note: Lamb shanks are commonly found in frozen bulk packages. If using frozen shanks, remember to thaw them before using.

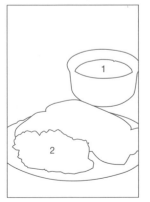

Variation: Lamb shoulder may be substituted, but the addition of the lamb bone provides extra richness.

1. Café au Lait Custard, page 133
2. French Lamb Casserole, above

Rosemary Lamb Shanks

Pair this aromatic lamb with hearty red wine, garlic mashed potatoes and a crisp green salad, and you'll be transported to a bistro in southern France.

Lamb shanks (about 3 – 4 lbs., 1.4 – 1.8 kg), see Note	6	6
Sliced onion	4 cups	1 L
Can of tomato paste	5 1/2 oz.	156 mL
Dry (or alcohol-free) red wine	1 cup	250 mL
Sprigs of fresh rosemary (or 2 tsp., 10 mL, dried, crushed)	3	3

Heat large greased frying pan on medium-high. Add lamb shanks. Cook for about 8 minutes, turning occasionally, until browned on all sides. Arrange lamb shanks in 5 to 7 quart (5 to 7 L) slow cooker.

Add onion to same frying pan. Reduce heat to medium. Sprinkle generously with salt. Sprinkle with pepper. Cook for about 15 minutes, stirring often, until browned.

Add tomato paste. Heat and stir for 1 minute. Add wine. Heat and stir, scraping any brown bits from bottom of pan, until boiling. Add to slow cooker.

Add rosemary sprigs and 2 cups (500 mL) water. Cook, covered, on Low for 8 to 10 hours or on High for 4 to 5 hours. Transfer lamb shanks to large serving platter. Cover to keep warm. Remove and discard rosemary stems. Skim and discard fat from cooking liquid. Carefully process with hand blender or blender in batches until smooth (see Safety Tip). Makes about 5 cups (1.25 L) sauce. Serve with lamb shanks. Serves 6.

1 lamb shank with 1/4 cup (60 mL) sauce: 649 Calories; 31.4 g Total Fat (13.4 g Mono, 2.5 g Poly, 12.9 g Sat); 240 mg Cholesterol; 15 g Carbohydrate; 3 g Fibre; 66 g Protein; 381 mg Sodium

Note: Lamb shanks are commonly found in frozen bulk packages. If using frozen shanks, remember to thaw them before using.

Safety Tip: Follow manufacturer's instructions for processing hot liquids.

Mushroom Pork Marsala

Tender meat infused with the deep, earthy flavours of mushroom and wine.
This rich and decadent dish tastes best spooned over egg noodles or potatoes.

Boneless pork shoulder butt steak, trimmed of fat, cut into 3/4 inch (2 cm) pieces	2 lbs.	900 g
Fresh brown (or white) mushrooms, quartered	2 cups	500 mL
Marsala wine	1 cup	250 mL
Can of condensed cream of wild mushroom soup	10 oz.	284 mL
Package of wild mushroom roast gravy sauce mix	1 oz.	30 g

Heat large greased frying pan on medium-high. Cook pork, in 2 batches, for about 5 minutes, stirring occasionally, until browned. Transfer to 3 1/2 to 4 quart (3.5 to 4 L) slow cooker.

Add mushrooms and Marsala to same frying pan. Heat and stir, scraping any brown bits from bottom of pan, until boiling. Add to slow cooker.

Add soup, gravy mix and 1/2 cup (125 mL) water to slow cooker. Stir. Cook, covered, on Low for 8 to 10 hours or on High for 4 to 5 hours. Makes about 4 cups (1 L).

1/2 cup (125 mL): 280 Calories; 14.2 g Total Fat (5.4 g Mono, 1.2 g Poly, 4.6 g Sat); 69 mg Cholesterol; 9 g Carbohydrate; trace Fibre; 21 g Protein; 503 mg Sodium

Pictured on page 107.

Paré Pointer
Spirits never buy lottery tickets—they don't have a ghost of a chance of winning.

Fruity Lamb Stew

North African tagines *are stews named for the clay-based, cone-shaped vessels in which they are cooked. Serve this sweet, rich-textured slow cooker version with couscous or rice.*

Boneless lamb shoulder, trimmed of fat, cut into 1 1/2 inch (3.8 cm) pieces	3 lbs.	1.4 kg
Mixed dried fruit (such as apricots, prunes, and apples), larger pieces cut in half	1 1/2 cups	375 mL
Pumpkin pie spice	1 tbsp.	15 mL
Envelope of roast gravy mix	1 1/8 oz.	32 g
Whole natural almonds, toasted (see Note)	1 cup	250 mL

Heat large well-greased frying pan on medium-high. Cook lamb, in 3 batches, sprinkling each batch with salt and pepper, for about 5 minutes, stirring occasionally, until browned. Transfer to 3 1/2 to 4 quart (3.5 to 4 L) slow cooker.

Add fruit and pumpkin pie spice. Stir.

Combine gravy mix and 2 cups (500 mL) water in medium bowl. Pour over lamb mixture. Cook, covered, on Low for 6 to 7 hours or on High for 3 to 3 1/2 hours.

Add almonds. Stir gently. Makes about 6 cups (1.5 L).

3/4 cup (175 mL): 483 Calories; 34.3 g Total Fat (10.4 g Mono, 2.4 g Poly, 9.9 g Sat); 123 mg Cholesterol; 6 g Carbohydrate; 2 g Fibre; 36 g Protein; 348 mg Sodium

Note: To toast the almonds, spread evenly in an ungreased shallow pan. Bake at 350°F (175°C) oven for 5 to 10 minutes, stirring or shaking often, until skins darken slighlty.

Barbecue Apple Chops

Baked potatoes are the perfect accompaniment for moist and tangy pork chops paired with a sweet barbecue sauce.

Bone-in pork chops, trimmed of fat	8	8
Chopped onion	1 cup	250 mL
Barbecue sauce, divided	1 cup	250 mL
Can of kernel corn	7 oz.	199 mL
Thinly sliced peeled tart apple (such as Granny Smith)	1 1/2 cups	375 mL

Heat large well-greased frying pan on medium-high. Cook pork chops, in 2 batches, for about 2 minutes per side until browned. Transfer to 5 to 7 quart (5 to 7 L) slow cooker.

Add onion to same greased frying pan. Reduce heat to medium. Cook for about 5 minutes, stirring often, until softened. Spread evenly over pork chops.

Drizzle 3/4 cup (175 mL) barbecue sauce over onion. Layer corn and apple over top, in order given. Drizzle with remaining barbecue sauce. Do not stir. Cook, covered, on Low for 6 to 7 hours or on High for 3 to 3 1/2 hours. Transfer pork chops to large serving platter. Makes about 2 1/3 cups (575 mL) sauce. Serve with pork chops.

1 serving with 1/3 cup (75 mL) sauce: 254 Calories; 13.0 g Total Fat (6.0 g Mono, 1.7 g Poly, 3.9 g Sat); 61 mg Cholesterol; 13 g Carbohydrate; 2 g Fibre; 20 g Protein; 388 mg Sodium

West Indies Rice Casserole

Salty ham bites are nicely balanced with sweet potato and spicy jerk seasoning in this fluffy rice dish. Stir the ham in at the end of cooking to distribute it and the sweet potato evenly.

Prepared chicken broth	2 cups	500 mL
Jerk seasoning paste	1 tbsp.	15 mL
Cubed fresh peeled orange-fleshed sweet potato	2 cups	500 mL
Long grain white rice	2 cups	500 mL
Ham steak (about 1 lb., 454 g), cut into quarters	1	1

Whisk broth and jerk paste in 4 to 5 quart (4 to 5 L) slow cooker until smooth. Add sweet potato, rice, 1 cup (250 mL) water and a sprinkle of salt and pepper. Stir.

Heat large greased frying pan on medium-high. Add ham. Cook for about 1 minute per side until starting to brown. Place over rice mixture. Cook, covered, on Low for 5 to 6 hours or on High for 2 1/2 to 3 hours. Transfer ham to work surface. Dice. Return to slow cooker. Stir gently. Makes about 7 cups (1.75 L).

1 cup (250 mL): 336 Calories; 4.2 g Total Fat (1.9 g Mono, 0.7 g Poly, 1.2 g Sat); 29 mg Cholesterol; 54 g Carbohydrate; 2 g Fibre; 18 g Protein; 1472 mg Sodium

Paré Pointer

If a rocket hits your foot, you have mistletoe.

Curried Lamb Shanks

Rustic lamb shanks are the perfect cut to slow cook with fragrant curry and sweet potato—and there's plenty of rich sauce to spoon over rice or cooked veggies.

Lamb shanks (about 3 to 4 lbs., 1.4 – 1.8 kg),see Note	6	6
Hot curry paste, divided	3 tbsp.	50 mL
Envelope of onion soup mix	1 1/4 oz.	38 g
Fresh peeled orange-fleshed sweet potato, cut into 1 inch (2.5 cm) pieces	2 lbs.	900 g
Ketchup	1 tbsp.	15 mL

Rub lamb shanks with 2 tbsp. (30 mL) curry paste. Sprinkle generously with pepper. Heat large well-greased frying pan on medium-high. Add lamb shanks. Cook for about 8 minutes, turning occasionally, until browned on all sides. Transfer to 5 to 7 quart (5 to 7 L) slow cooker.

Combine soup mix and 2 cups (500 mL) water in small bowl. Add to slow cooker. Stir. Cook, covered, on Low for 6 hours or on High for 3 hours.

Add sweet potato. Cook, covered, on High for 1 1/2 to 2 hours until lamb shanks and sweet potato are tender. Transfer lamb shanks to serving bowl. Cover to keep warm. Transfer all but 1/2 cup (125 mL) sweet potato with slotted spoon to separate serving bowl. Cover to keep warm. Skim and discard fat from cooking liquid.

Transfer remaining liquid and sweet potato to blender. Add remaining curry paste and ketchup. Carefully process in batches until smooth (see Safety Tip). Pour over lamb. Serves 6.

1 serving: 375 Calories; 14.3 g Total Fat (5.8 g Mono, 1.4 g Poly, 5.0 g Sat); 80 mg Cholesterol; 36 g Carbohydrate; 5 g Fibre; 24 g Protein; 956 mg Sodium

Note: Lamb shanks are commonly found in frozen bulk packages. If using frozen shanks, remember to thaw them before using.

Safety Tip: Follow manufacturer's instructions for processing hot liquids.

Peachy Ribs

Enjoy the flavours of tender, barbecue-flavoured pork ribs with a touch of summery peach sweetness. Drizzle the smooth, tasty sauce over the ribs for even more flavour.

Pork side ribs, trimmed of fat and cut into 3-bone portions	3 lbs.	1.4 kg
All-purpose flour	1/4 cup	60 mL
Can of sliced peaches, drained and juice reserved, chopped	14 oz.	398 mL
Barbecue sauce	1/4 cup	60 mL
Peach jam	1/4 cup	60 mL

Sprinkle ribs with salt and pepper. Put into large resealable freezer bag. Add flour. Seal bag. Turn until coated. Put ribs into 3 1/2 to 4 quart (3.5 to 4 L) slow cooker.

Spoon peaches over top. Combine barbecue sauce, jam and reserved peach juice in small bowl. Pour over peaches. Cook, covered, on Low for 8 to 10 hours or on High for 4 to 5 hours. Transfer ribs to large serving platter. Cover to keep warm. Skim and discard fat from cooking liquid. Carefully process in blender until smooth (see Safety Tip). Pour sauce over ribs. Makes ten 3-bone portions.

1 portion: 558 Calories; 40.4 g Total Fat (18.4 g Mono, 3.2 g Poly, 15.0 g Sat); 161 mg Cholesterol; 13 g Carbohydrate; 1 g Fibre; 33 g Protein; 250 mg Sodium

Safety Tip: Follow manufacturer's instructions for processing hot liquids.

Cauliflower Potato Scallop

This rich and creamy scallop is a decadent way to eat your vegetables. It's full of creamy Alfredo sauce and tender kale, potato and cauliflower.

Alfredo pasta sauce	2 cups	500 mL
Thinly sliced peeled potato	5 cups	1.25 L
Chopped kale leaves, lightly packed (see Tip, below)	3 cups	750 mL
Cauliflower florets	3 cups	750 mL
Grated Parmesan cheese	1 cup	250 mL

Combine pasta sauce and 1 cup (250 mL) water in small bowl.

To assemble, layer ingredients in well-greased 4 to 5 quart (4 to 5 L) slow cooker as follows:

1. Half of potato
2. Half of kale
3. Half of cauliflower
4. Half of sauce mixture
5. Half of cheese
6. Remaining potato
7. Remaining kale
8. Remaining cauliflower
9. Remaining sauce mixture
10. Remaining cheese

Cook, covered, on Low for 8 to 9 hours or on High for 4 to 4 1/2 hours. Makes about 10 cups (2.5 L).

1 cup (250 mL): 261 Calories; 11.9 g Total Fat (trace Mono, 0.2 g Poly, 5.3 g Sat); 32 mg Cholesterol; 31 g Carbohydrate; 4 g Fibre; 10 g Protein; 778 mg Sodium

 To remove the centre rib from lettuce or kale, fold the leaf in half along the rib and then cut along the length of the rib. To store, place leaves in large freezer bag. Once frozen, crumble in bag.

Stuffed Cabbage Wraps

An easy version of traditional cabbage rolls, these rice and bean wraps have great tomato taste. Try serving them as a side.

Large head of green cabbage	1	1
Chopped onion	3/4 cup	175 mL
Cooked long-grain brown rice (about 1/2 cup, 125 mL, uncooked)	1 1/2 cups	375 mL
Can of black beans, rinsed and drained	19 oz.	540 mL
Tomato pasta sauce	3 cups	750 mL

Remove core from cabbage. Trim about 1/2 inch (12 mm) slice from bottom. Place, cut-side down, in 4 to 5 quart (4 to 5 L) slow cooker. Cover with boiling water. Let stand, covered, for 5 minutes. Drain. Let stand until cool enough to handle. Carefully remove 8 large outer leaves from cabbage (see Note). Cut "V" shape along tough ribs of leaves to remove. Discard ribs. Set leaves aside.

Heat medium greased frying pan on medium. Add onion. Cook for about 5 minutes, stirring often, until starting to soften. Transfer to medium bowl.

Add rice, beans, 1/2 cup (125 mL) pasta sauce and a sprinkle of salt and pepper. Stir. Place about 1/3 cup (75 mL) rice mixture on 1 cabbage leaf. Fold in sides. Roll up tightly from bottom to enclose filling. Repeat with remaining rice mixture and cabbage leaves. Pour remaining pasta sauce into slow cooker. Arrange cabbage rolls in 2 layers, seam-side down, over sauce. Cook, covered, on Low for 7 to 8 hours or High for 3 1/2 to 4 hours. Transfer rolls with slotted spoon to serving plate. Serve with sauce. Makes 1 1/2 cups (375 mL) sauce and 8 rolls.

1 cabbage roll with 3 tbsp. (50 mL) sauce: 263 Calories; 4.1 g Total Fat (0.7 g Mono, 1.1 g Poly, 0.3 g Sat); 0 mg Cholesterol; 46 g Carbohydrate; 7 g Fibre; 9 g Protein; 643 mg Sodium

Note: Discard any other outer leaves that are partially steamed. Save the remaining cabbage in the refrigerator for another use.

African Quinoa Stew

Quinoa (KEEN-wah), beans and peanut butter are a delicious, creative combination that packs a protein punch in this rich and colourful African-inspired stew.

Chopped onion	1 1/2 cups	375 mL
Cans of red kidney beans (19 oz., 540 mL, each), rinsed and drained	2	2
Tomato sauce	2 cups	500 mL
Quinoa, rinsed and drained	1 cup	250 mL
Peanut butter	6 tbsp.	100 mL

Heat large greased frying pan on medium. Add onion. Cook for about 8 minutes, stirring often, until softened. Transfer to 3 1/2 to 4 quart (3.5 to 4 L) slow cooker.

Add remaining 4 ingredients, 1 cup (250 mL) water and a generous sprinkle of salt and pepper. Stir. Cook, covered, on Low for 5 to 6 hours or on High for 2 1/2 to 3 hours. Makes about 8 cups (2 L).

1 cup (250 mL): 348 Calories; 8.9 g Total Fat (0.7 g Mono, 0.7 g Poly, 1.5 g Sat); 0 mg Cholesterol; 53 g Carbohydrate; 15 g Fibre; 17 g Protein; 547 mg Sodium

Pineapple Bean Bake

These smoky, sweet and tangy beans would make a great side at your next barbecue—spoon some up with a steak hot from the grill.

Cans of red kidney beans (19 oz., 540 mL, each), rinsed and drained	2	2
Cans of baked beans in tomato sauce (14 oz., 398 mL, each)	2	2
Can of crushed pineapple (with juice)	19 oz.	540 mL
Finely chopped onion	1 cup	250 mL
Hickory barbecue sauce	1/2 cup	125 mL

Combine all 5 ingredients in 3 1/2 to 4 quart (3.5 to 4 L) slow cooker. Cook, covered, on Low for 8 to 9 hours or on High for 4 to 4 1/2 hours. Makes about 8 1/2 cups (2.1 L).

1 cup (250 mL): 294 Calories; 1.2 g Total Fat (0.1 g Mono, 0.1 g Poly, trace Sat); 0 mg Cholesterol; 58 g Carbohydrate; 17 g Fibre; 14 g Protein; 471 mg Sodium

Chickpea Lentil Stew

Come home to hearty lentils and chickpeas brightened with the fresh flavours of tomatoes, garlic and feta. Fresh basil can be used as an additional garnish.

Cans of chickpeas (garbanzo beans), 19 oz. (540 mL) each, rinsed and drained	2	2
Cans of lentils (19 oz., 540 mL, each), rinsed and drained	2	2
Diced peeled potato	2 cups	500 mL
Prepared bruschetta topping	2 cups	500 mL
Crumbled feta cheese	1 cup	250 mL

Combine first 3 ingredients and 2 cups (500 mL) water in 4 to 5 quart (4 to 5 L) slow cooker. Cook, covered, on Low for 6 to 8 hours or on High for 3 to 4 hours. Mash mixture several times with potato masher to break up potato.

Add bruschetta topping and feta cheese. Stir. Makes about 11 cups (2.75 L).

1 cup (250 mL): 298 Calories; 8.3 g Total Fat (1.1 g Mono, 1.1 g Poly, 2.1 g Sat); 12 mg Cholesterol; 47 g Carbohydrate; 9 g Fibre; 16 g Protein; 620 mg Sodium

Barley Primavera

Creamy and appealing, this comfort food has a risotto-like texture and lots of colourful, tender-crisp vegetables, with the added nutritional value of barley.

Prepared vegetable broth	4 cups	1 L
Pot barley	2 cups	500 mL
Frozen Italian mixed vegetables, thawed	4 cups	1 L
Alfredo pasta sauce	1 2/3 cups	400 mL
Prepared bruschetta topping	1 1/2 cups	375 mL

Combine broth, barley and 2 cups (500 mL) water in 4 to 5 quart (4 to 5 L) slow cooker. Cook, covered, on Low for 5 to 6 hours or on High for 2 1/2 to 3 hours until barley is tender and liquid is absorbed.

(continued on next page)

Add vegetables and pasta sauce. Stir. Cook, covered, on High for about 30 minutes until vegetables are tender.

Add bruschetta topping. Stir. Makes about 12 cups (3 L).

1 cup (250 mL): 270 Calories; 12.7 g Total Fat (0 g Mono, 0 g Poly, 5.8 g Sat); 31 mg Cholesterol; 34 g Carbohydrate; 6 g Fibre; 6 g Protein; 577 mg Sodium

Pictured on page 125.

Meatless Moussaka

Lentils replace the meat in this comforting Greek dish with simple and distinct tastes. For less fuss and more flavour, the traditional béchamel topping was traded up for a quick and easy sprinkle of creamy goat cheese.

Cans of lentils (19 oz., 540 mL, each), rinsed and drained	2	2
Tomato pasta sauce	3 cups	750 mL
Ground cinnamon	1/4 tsp.	1 mL
Medium eggplants (with peel), cut into 1/4 inch (6 mm) slices	2	2
Goat (chèvre) cheese, crumbled	8 oz.	225 g

Combine first 3 ingredients and a sprinkle of salt and pepper in large bowl.

To assemble, layer ingredients in greased 5 to 7 quart (5 to 7 L) slow cooker as follows:

1. 2 cups (500 mL) lentil mixture
2. Half of eggplant
3. 2 cups (500 mL) lentil mixture
4. Remaining eggplant
5. Remaining lentil mixture

Cook, covered, on Low for 8 to 9 hours or on High for 4 to 4 1/2 hours.

Sprinkle with cheese. Cook, covered, on High for about 10 minutes until cheese is softened. Makes about 9 cups (2.25 L).

1 cup (250 mL): 257 Calories; 6.5 g Total Fat (1.4 g Mono, 0.5 g Poly, 3.8 g Sat); 12 mg Cholesterol; 42 g Carbohydrate; 9 g Fibre; 18 g Protein; 386 mg Sodium

Ratatouille

This great vegetarian entree can be served on creamy polenta or a bed of rice. A versatile dish, ratatouille (ra-tuh-TOO-ee) also makes a hearty pasta sauce or a great side dish for roasted meats.

Chopped eggplant (with peel), 1 inch (2.5 cm) pieces	8 cups	2 L
Chopped yellow pepper (1 inch, 2.5 cm, pieces)	5 cups	1.25 L
Chopped zucchini (with peel), 1 inch (2.5 cm) pieces	5 cups	1.25 L
Can of spicy tomato sauce	25 oz.	680 mL
Basil pesto	2 tbsp.	30 mL

Spread eggplant evenly on well-greased baking sheet with sides. Sprinkle with salt and pepper. Toss until coated. Broil on top rack in oven, stirring occasionally, for about 10 minutes until browned. Transfer to 5 to 7 quart (5 to 7 L) slow cooker.

Add next 3 ingredients. Stir. Cook, covered, on Low for 6 to 8 hours or on High for 3 to 4 hours.

Add pesto. Stir. Makes about 11 1/2 cups (2.9 L).

1 cup (250 mL): 109 Calories; 5.4 g Total Fat (1.5 g Mono, 1.4 g Poly, 0.8 g Sat); 2 mg Cholesterol; 14 g Carbohydrate; 4 g Fibre; 4 g Protein; 330 mg Sodium

Pictured on page 125.

Squash and Couscous

This comforting dish has the earthiness of squash and the sweetness of apricot, all with an eastern Mediterranean flair.

Chopped dried apricot	2/3 cup	150 mL
Cubed butternut squash (1 inch, 2.5 cm, pieces)	6 cups	1.5 L
Butter (or hard margarine), melted	2 tbsp.	30 mL
Box of lemon and spinach couscous	7 oz.	198 g
Pine nuts, toasted (see Tip, page 146)	2 tbsp.	30 mL

(continued on next page)

122 Main Courses - Vegetarian

Combine apricot and 1 1/2 cups (375 mL) boiling water in small bowl. Let stand for 10 minutes. Drain, reserving 1 cup (250 mL) water. Transfer apricot to greased 4 to 5 quart (4 to 5 L) slow cooker.

Add squash. Drizzle with melted butter. Sprinkle with salt and pepper. Stir well. Cook, covered, on Low for 6 to 7 hours or on High for 3 to 3 1/2 hours until tender.

Combine couscous and reserved water. Add to squash mixture. Stir gently. Cook, covered, on High for about 10 minutes until couscous is tender and liquid is absorbed.

Sprinkle with pine nuts. Makes about 7 cups (1.75 L).

1 cup (250 mL): 270 Calories; 5.7 g Total Fat (1.3 g Mono, 1.0 g Poly, 2.2 g Sat); 9 mg Cholesterol; 54 g Carbohydrate; 6 g Fibre; 7 g Protein; 375 mg Sodium

Salsa Veggie Chili

This is an easy vegetarian chili with delicious, crowd-pleasing results. Tasty with tortilla chips or crusty bread for dipping.

Can of kidney beans, rinsed and drained	19 oz.	540 mL
Chunky salsa	2 cups	500 mL
Tomato sauce	2 cups	500 mL
Package of veggie ground round (see Note)	12 oz.	340 g
Chili powder	2 tsp.	10 mL

Combine all 5 ingredients in 3 1/2 to 4 quart (3.5 to 4 L) slow cooker. Cook, covered, on Low for 7 to 8 hours or on High for 3 1/2 to 4 hours. Makes about 6 cups (1.5 L).

1 cup (250 mL): 184 Calories; 0 g Total Fat (0 g Mono, 0 g Poly, 0 g Sat); 0 mg Cholesterol; 30 g Carbohydrate; 7 g Fibre; 16 g Protein; 1442 mg Sodium

Note: Veggie ground round is available in the produce section of your grocery store.

Vegetable Curry

Indian-inspired flavours are now available in convenient cooking sauces, perfect for use in a slow cooker. Serve this curry over coconut rice, and garnish with chopped cilantro for extra colour.

Chopped butternut squash (1 inch, 2.5 cm, pieces)	4 cups	1 L
Cauliflower florets	3 cups	750 mL
Baby potatoes, cut in half	1 lb.	454 g
Jar of tikka masala cooking sauce (see Note)	14 oz.	400 mL
Can of diced tomatoes (with juice)	14 oz.	398 mL

Combine first 3 ingredients and 1/2 cup (125 mL) water in 3 1/2 to 4 quart (3.5 to 4 L) slow cooker. Cook, covered, on Low for 6 to 7 hours or on High for 3 to 3 1/2 hours until tender.

Add tikka masala sauce and tomatoes. Stir. Cook, covered, on High for about 30 minutes until heated through. Makes about 7 cups (1.75 L).

1 cup (250 mL): 407 Calories; 24.1 g Total Fat (trace Mono, 0.1 g Poly, 2.0 g Sat); 0 mg Cholesterol; 43 g Carbohydrate; 6 g Fibre; 7 g Protein; 2342 mg Sodium

Note: Canned curry sauce that requires the addition of water can also be used, as long as the final volume equals 14 oz. (400 mL).

1. Classic "Baked" Beans, page 127
2. Ratatouille, page 122
3. Barley Primavera, page 120

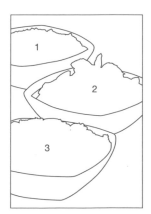

Classic "Baked" Beans

Cooking dry beans in a slow cooker is not only easy, but healthy and inexpensive, too! Serve these beans with buttered biscuits or freeze in small portions.

Dried navy beans	5 cups	1.25 L
Chopped onion	1 cup	250 mL
Ketchup	1 1/2 cups	375 mL
Fancy (mild) molasses	1/3 cup	75 mL
Prepared mustard	2 tbsp.	30 mL

Measure beans into large bowl or Dutch oven. Add water until 2 inches (5 cm) above beans. Soak overnight (see Tip, page 15). Drain. Rinse beans. Drain. Transfer to 5 to 7 quart (5 to 7 L) slow cooker.

Add onion and 5 cups (1.25 L) water. Cook, covered, on High for 4 to 4 1/2 hours until beans are tender (see Note).

Add remaining 3 ingredients and a generous sprinkle of salt and pepper. Stir. Cook, covered, on High for 30 minutes. Sprinkle generously with salt and pepper. Stir. Makes about 12 cups (3 L).

1 cup (250 mL): 206 Calories; 0.5 g Total Fat (0.1 g Mono, 0.2 g Poly, 0.1 g Sat); 0 mg Cholesterol; 45 g Carbohydrate; 6 g Fibre; 8 g Protein; 939 mg Sodium

Pictured on page 125.

Note: Cooking beans on Low setting is not recommended as they may not cook fully.

1. White Bean Vegetable Chili, page 132
2. Pineapple Cherry Cobbler, page 136

Jamaican Rice and Beans

This creamy, mildly seasoned dish can be served as a vegetarian main course or as a side. Though pigeon peas are used in the most authentic Jamaican rice dishes, kidney beans are frequently substituted.

Chopped onion	1 cup	250 mL
Cans of red kidney beans (14 oz., 398 mL each), rinsed and drained	2	2
Long-grain brown rice	2 cups	500 mL
Ground allspice	1 tsp.	5 mL
Can of coconut milk	14 oz.	398 mL

Heat medium greased frying pan on medium. Add onion and a generous sprinkle of salt and pepper. Cook for about 5 minutes, stirring often, until softened. Transfer to 4 to 5 quart (4 to 5 L) slow cooker.

Add next 4 ingredients, 2 1/4 cups (550 mL) water and a generous sprinkle of salt and pepper. Stir. Cook, covered, on Low for 6 to 7 hours or on High for 3 to 3 1/2 hours. Makes about 8 cups (2 L).

1 cup (250 mL): 363 Calories; 12.6 g Total Fat (1.3 g Mono, 0.8 g Poly, 9.7 g Sat); 0 mg Cholesterol; 54 g Carbohydrate; 8 g Fibre; 11 g Protein; 413 mg Sodium

Simple Dal

This colourful South Asian dish goes easy on the spices, and is delicious served over rice or with flatbread. For more adventurous palates, add another tablespoon of curry paste or use hot paste instead of mild.

Chopped onion	1 cup	250 mL
Dried red split lentils	2 1/2 cups	625 mL
Mild curry paste	3 tbsp.	50 mL
Can of diced tomatoes, drained	14 oz.	398 mL
Chopped fresh cilantro (or parsley)	1/2 cup	125 mL

Heat medium greased frying pan on medium. Add onion. Cook for about 5 minutes, stirring often, until softened. Transfer to 3 1/2 to 4 quart (3.5 to 4 L) slow cooker.

(continued on next page)

Add lentils, curry paste and 5 1/2 cups (1.4 L) water. Stir. Cook, covered, on Low for 6 to 7 hours or High for 3 to 3 1/2 hours.

Add tomatoes and a generous sprinkle of salt. Stir. Cook, covered, on High for about 10 minutes until heated through.

Add cilantro. Stir. Makes about 8 cups (2 L).

1 cup (250 mL): 252 Calories; 3.0 g Total Fat (0.3 g Mono, 0.2 g Poly, 0.4 g Sat); 0 mg Cholesterol; 40 g Carbohydrate; 9 g Fibre; 17 g Protein; 467 mg Sodium

---

Veggie Pasta Sauce

This easy-to-prepare pasta sauce has a hearty, meaty texture, but without the meat. It's perfect on pasta and can be used to make lasagna.

Tomato basil pasta sauce	4 cups	1 L
Package of veggie ground round (see Note)	12 oz.	340 g
Chopped carrot	1 cup	250 mL
Chopped onion	1 cup	250 mL
Chopped zucchini (with peel)	1 cup	250 mL

Combine all 5 ingredients in 3 1/2 to 4 quart (3.5 to 4 L) slow cooker. Cook, covered, on Low for 7 to 8 hours or on High for 3 1/2 to 4 hours. Makes about 6 cups (1.5 L).

3/4 cup (175 mL): 144 Calories; 2.6 g Total Fat (trace Mono, trace Poly, trace Sat); 0 mg Cholesterol; 17 g Carbohydrate; 3 g Fibre; 11 g Protein; 692 mg Sodium

Pictured on page 90.

Note: Veggie ground round is available in the produce section of your grocery store.

Curried Cauliflower Paneer

The spinach contrasts beautifully with curry-coated cauliflower and paneer in this mild vegetarian dish that's best served over basmati rice. Garnish with a dollop of plain thick yogurt and cilantro sprigs.

Can of tikka masala curry sauce (see Note)	10 oz.	284 mL
Cauliflower florets	4 cups	1 L
Cubed paneer	3 cups	750 mL
Fresh spinach leaves, lightly packed	4 cups	1 L
Chopped fresh cilantro (or parsley)	1 tbsp.	15 mL

Combine curry sauce and 1 cup (250 mL) water in 3 1/2 to 4 quart (3.5 to 4 L) slow cooker. Add cauliflower, paneer and a generous sprinkle of salt. Stir. Cook, covered, on Low for 5 to 6 hours or on High for 2 1/2 to 3 hours.

Add spinach, cilantro and a sprinkle of salt and pepper. Stir. Makes about 6 cups (1.5 L).

1 cup (250 mL): 621 Calories; 50.5 g Total Fat (0 g Mono, trace Poly, 21.6 g Sat); 120 mg Cholesterol; 12 g Carbohydrate; 1 g Fibre; 29 g Protein; 2126 mg Sodium

Note: Jarred cooking sauce, which does not require the addition of water, may be used. Omit water and use 2 1/4 cups (550 mL) cooking sauce.

Black Beans and Barley

Flavourful onion and a mild malt taste make this combination of black beans and tender barley a treat—tastes great with a crisp side salad.

Prepared vegetable broth	3 cups	750 mL
Pot barley	2 cups	500 mL
Can of beer	12 1/2 oz.	355 mL
Envelope of onion soup mix	1 1/4 oz.	38 g
Cans of black beans (19 oz., 540 mL, each), rinsed and drained	2	2

Combine first 4 ingredients and 1 1/2 cups (375 mL) water in 4 to 5 quart (4 to 5 L) slow cooker. Cook, covered, on Low for 5 to 6 hours or on High for 2 1/2 to 3 hours until barley is tender and liquid is absorbed.

(continued on next page)

Add beans. Stir. Cook, covered, on High for 10 minutes until heated through. Makes about 11 cups (2.75 L).

1 cup (250 mL): 246 Calories; 1.8 g Total Fat (0.1 g Mono, 0.8 g Poly, trace Sat); trace Cholesterol; 45 g Carbohydrate; 12 g Fibre; 10 g Protein; 723 mg Sodium

---

Veggie Shepherd's Pie

A hearty vegetarian dish with the comforting flavours of home, this slow cooker casserole has a nice blend of seasonings and a hint of spicy heat.

Packages of veggie ground round (12 oz., 340 g, each), see Note	2	2
Prepared bruschetta topping	1 1/2 cups	375 mL
Frozen peas, thawed	1 cup	250 mL
Can of kernel corn, drained	7 oz.	199 mL
Mashed potatoes (about 2 lbs., 900 g, uncooked)	4 1/2 cups	1.1 L

Combine first 3 ingredients in 3 1/2 to 4 quart (3.5 to 4 L) slow cooker.

Scatter corn over ground round mixture. Do not stir. Sprinkle mashed potatoes with salt and pepper. Stir. Spread mashed potatoes over corn. Do not stir. Lay double layer of tea towel over slow cooker liner. Cover with lid. Cook on Low for 6 to 7 hours or on High for 3 to 3 1/2 hours. Makes about 10 cups (2.5 L).

1 cup (250 mL): 217 Calories; 2.9 g Total Fat (0 g Mono, trace Poly, trace Sat); 0 mg Cholesterol; 32 g Carbohydrate; 7 g Fibre; 15 g Protein; 902 mg Sodium

Note: Veggie ground round is available in the produce section of your grocery store.

Paré Pointer

Goats have no manners—they butt in all the time.

White Bean Vegetable Chili

This hearty bean chili is quick to put together, and can be used as a taco filling too! Add your favourite mixed veggies and serve with tortilla chips or corn bread.

Cans of white kidney beans (19 oz., 540 mL, each), rinsed and drained	2	2
Cans of stewed tomatoes (14 oz., 398 mL, each), cut up	2	2
Prepared vegetable broth	1 cup	250 mL
Envelope of chili seasoning mix	1 1/4 oz.	35 g
Frozen mixed vegetables, thawed	3 cups	750 mL

Combine first 4 ingredients in 3 1/2 to 4 quart (3.5 to 4 L) slow cooker. Cook, covered, on Low for 6 to 8 hours or on High for 3 to 4 hours.

Add vegetables. Stir. Cook, covered, on High for about 30 minutes until vegetables are tender. Makes about 7 cups (1.75 L).

1 cup (250 mL): 206 Calories; 4.2 g Total Fat (0 g Mono, 0 g Poly, 1.0 g Sat); 4 mg Cholesterol; 34 g Carbohydrate; 7 g Fibre; 10 g Protein; 630 mg Sodium

Pictured on page 126.

Lentil Pasta Sauce

A pasta sauce that will satisfy the family and add a vegetarian meal option to your weekly menu. Complete the meal with a salad and garlic bread.

Diced zucchini (with peel)	2 cups	500 mL
Chopped onion	1 cup	250 mL
Grated carrot	1 cup	250 mL
Roasted garlic tomato pasta sauce	6 cups	1.5 L
Can of lentils, rinsed and drained	19 oz.	540 mL

Heat large greased frying pan on medium. Add first 3 ingredients. Cook for about 10 minutes, stirring often, until onion is softened and starts to brown. Transfer to 3 1/2 to 4 quart (3.5 to 4 L) slow cooker.

Add pasta sauce and lentils. Stir. Cook, covered, on Low for 6 to 8 hours or on High for 3 to 4 hours. Makes about 9 cups (2.25 L).

3/4 cup (175 mL): 114 Calories; 1.2 g Total Fat (0.3 g Mono, 0.2 g Poly, 0.1 g Sat); 0 mg Cholesterol; 23 g Carbohydrate; 2 g Fibre; 6 g Protein; 334 mg Sodium

Café au Lait Custard

*Rich, coffee-flavoured baked custard is a smooth, sweet ending
to a meal. Whether you serve it warm or chilled, a dollop of whipped cream
is the perfect garnish.*

Large eggs	3	3
Granulated sugar	1/2 cup	125 mL
Vanilla extract	1 tsp.	5 mL
Can of evaporated milk	13 1/2 oz.	385 mL
Instant coffee granules	1 1/2 tbsp.	25 mL

Whisk first 3 ingredients and a sprinkle of salt in medium heatproof bowl
until smooth.

Combine milk and coffee granules in medium saucepan on medium. Heat
for about 5 minutes, stirring often, until coffee granules are dissolved and
bubbles form around edge of saucepan. Slowly add to egg mixture, stirring
constantly, until sugar is dissolved. Strain mixture through sieve back into
pan. Pour mixture into 4 greased 3/4 cup (175 mL) ovenproof ramekins.
Put an even layer (2 to 3 inches, 5 to 7.5 cm, thick) of crumpled foil into
bottom of 5 to 7 quart (5 to 7 L) slow cooker (see Tip, page 80). Place
ramekins on foil, pushing down gently to settle evenly. Pour hot water into
slow cooker until halfway up side of ramekins. Lay double layer of tea towel
over slow cooker liner. Cover with lid. Cook on High for about 1 1/2 hours
until custard is set. Serves 4.

*1 serving: 276 Calories; 9.5 g Total Fat (1.3 g Mono, 0.3 g Poly, 5.7 g Sat); 192 mg Cholesterol;
35 g Carbohydrate; 0 g Fibre; 11 g Protein; 286 mg Sodium*

Pictured on page 108.

Steamed Pumpkin Carrot Cake

This spicy snack cake is really easy to prepare. If desired, ice with prepared cream cheese frosting, drizzle with caramel sauce, or dust with icing sugar.

Carrot muffin mix	2 cups	500 mL
Ground cinnamon	1 tsp.	5 mL
Canned pumpkin pie filling	1 cup	250 mL
Large eggs	2	2
Raisins	1/2 cup	125 mL

Combine muffin mix and cinnamon in large bowl. Make a well in centre.

Whisk pie filling, eggs and 2/3 cup (150 mL) water in medium bowl until smooth. Add raisins. Stir. Add to well. Stir until just moistened. Pour into greased 8 inch (20 cm) springform pan. Put an even layer (2 to 3 inches, 5 to 7.5 mL, thick) of crumpled foil into bottom of 5 to 7 quart (5 to 7 L) slow cooker (see Tip, page 80). Place pan on foil, pushing down gently to settle evenly. Lay double layer of tea towel over slow cooker liner. Cover with lid. Cook on High for about 2 1/2 hours until wooden pick inserted in centre comes out clean. Transfer pan to wire rack. Cool completely. Cuts into 12 wedges.

1 wedge: 163 Calories; 6.7 g Total Fat (0 g Mono, 0 g Poly, 6.2 g Sat); 36 mg Cholesterol; 29 g Carbohydrate; 17 g Fibre; 7 g Protein; 536 mg Sodium

Paré Pointer

Baby pigs eat constantly—they are trying to make hogs of themselves.

Winter's Day Compote

Gently cooked apple, apricot and raisins create a warm compote to serve alongside plain cheesecake or vanilla ice cream. If you have any leftovers, it makes a delicious addition to granola or oatmeal for breakfast.

Sliced peeled cooking apple (such as McIntosh)	3 cups	750 mL
Sliced peeled tart apple (such as Granny Smith)	3 cups	750 mL
Chopped dried apricot	1 cup	250 mL
Brown sugar, packed	1/3 cup	75 mL
Can of raisin pie filling	19 oz.	540 mL

Combine first 4 ingredients and 1 cup (250 mL) water in 3 1/2 to 4 quart (3.5 to 4 L) slow cooker.

Spoon pie filling over top. Do not stir. Cook, covered, on Low for 5 to 6 hours or on High for 2 1/2 to 3 hours. Stir. Makes about 6 1/2 cups (1.6 L).

1/2 cup (125 mL): 115 Calories; 0.1 g Total Fat (0 g Mono, trace Poly, trace Sat); 0 mg Cholesterol; 29 g Carbohydrate; 2 g Fibre; trace Protein; 46 mg Sodium

Raisin Bread Pudding

Bread pudding loaded with raisins, just like it should be! This pudding is especially nice if drizzled with maple syrup.

Large eggs	4	4
Milk	2 cups	500 mL
Brown sugar, packed	1/2 cup	125 mL
Ground cinnamon	1/2 tsp.	2 mL
Raisin bread cubes (about 8 slices)	9 cups	2.25 L

Beat eggs in large bowl until frothy. Add next 3 ingredients. Beat well.

Add bread cubes. Toss. Transfer to well-greased 3 1/2 to 4 quart (3.5 to 4 L) slow cooker. Cook, covered, on High for about 2 hours until firm. Serves 6.

1 serving: 248 Calories; 5.4 g Total Fat (1.1 g Mono, 0.2 g Poly, 1.9 g Sat); 148 mg Cholesterol; 41 g Carbohydrate; 2 g Fibre; 10 g Protein; 229 mg Sodium

Pineapple Cherry Cobbler

This easy cobbler has sweet cherry and pineapple flavours underneath a cake-like biscuit layer. Add a scoop of ice cream to each bowlful.

Can of cherry pie filling	19 oz.	540 mL
Can of crushed pineapple (with juice)	19 oz.	540 mL
Biscuit mix	1 1/2 cups	375 mL
Large egg, fork-beaten	1	1
Buttermilk (or soured milk), see Note	1 cup	250 mL

Combine pie filling and pineapple in greased 3 1/2 to 4 quart (3.5 to 4 L) slow cooker.

Measure biscuit mix into medium bowl. Make a well in centre.

Add egg and buttermilk to well. Stir until just moistened. Spoon evenly over pineapple mixture. Cook, covered, on High for 2 1/2 to 3 hours until wooden pick inserted in centre comes out clean. Serves 8.

1 serving: 233 Calories; 3.9 g Total Fat (0.2 g Mono, trace Poly, 1.2 g Sat); 29 mg Cholesterol; 45 g Carbohydrate; 1 g Fibre; 5 g Protein; 354 mg Sodium

Pictured on page 126.

Note: To make soured milk, measure 1 tbsp. (15 mL) white vinegar or lemon juice into a 1 cup (250 mL) liquid measure. Add enough milk to make 1 cup (250 mL). Stir. Let stand for 1 minute.

Oatmeal Cookie Crisp

Choose your favourite fruit to cook up in this easy dessert—try strawberries and rhubarb in season for a special treat. Serve it warm with a dollop of whipped cream, or spoon some over vanilla ice cream.

Fresh (or frozen, thawed) mixed berries	4 cups	1 L
Minute tapioca	3 tbsp.	50 mL
Crushed crisp oatmeal cookies (about 12)	1 1/2 cups	375 mL
Chopped pecans	1/2 cup	125 mL
Butter (or hard margarine), melted	2 tbsp.	30 mL

(continued on next page)

Combine berries and tapioca in greased 3 1/2 to 4 quart (3.5 to 4 L) slow cooker. Cook, covered, on Low for 3 hours or on High for 1 1/2 hours.

Combine remaining 3 ingredients in small bowl. Spoon over berry mixture. Do not stir. Lay double layer of tea towel over slow cooker liner. Cover with lid. Cook on High for about 30 minutes until browned and crisp. Makes about 4 cups (1 L).

1/2 cup (125 mL): 257 Calories; 14.6 g Total Fat (6.2 g Mono, 2.4 g Poly, 4.4 g Sat); 12 mg Cholesterol; 30 g Carbohydrate; 4 g Fibre; 3 g Protein; 150 mg Sodium

---

Danish Rice Pudding

This creamy pudding with tangy raspberry sauce is traditionally served at Christmastime in Denmark. It's customary to hide a whole blanched almond in the pudding. Whoever finds the almond in their serving wins a prize.

Can of sweetened condensed milk	11 oz.	300 mL
Arborio rice, rinsed and drained	1 cup	250 mL
Slivered almonds, toasted (see Tip, page 146)	3/4 cup	175 mL
Whipping cream, divided	2 cups	500 mL
Container of frozen raspberries in syrup, thawed	15 oz.	425 g

Combine condensed milk, rice and 2 1/4 cups (550 mL) water in well-greased 3 1/2 to 4 quart (3.5 to 4 L) slow cooker. Cook, covered, on Low for 4 hours or on High for 2 hours. Transfer rice mixture to large bowl. Let stand, uncovered, for 15 minutes.

Add almonds and 1/4 cup (60 mL) whipping cream. Stir. Chill, covered, for about 45 minutes, stirring occasionally, until cooled completely. Beat remaining whipping cream in medium bowl until stiff peaks form. Fold into rice mixture.

Put raspberries and syrup into medium saucepan. Cook, uncovered, on medium for about 10 minutes, stirring occasionally, until slightly reduced. Spoon over individual servings. Serves 8.

1 serving: 523 Calories; 30.2 g Total Fat (9.6 g Mono, 2.1 g Poly, 16.2 g Sat); 92 mg Cholesterol; 57 g Carbohydrate; 3 g Fibre; 8 g Protein; 82 mg Sodium

Pictured on page 143.

Fruity Chocolate Cake Dessert

A nice dark chocolate cake served up with saucy fruit—great for a winter dessert. A dollop of whipped cream would be a fine garnish.

Package of chocolate cake mix (1 layer size)	1	1
Large eggs, fork-beaten	2	2
Melted butter (or hard margarine), divided	1/2 cup	125 mL
Cans of fruit cocktail (14 oz., 398 mL, each), drained and juice reserved	2	2
Brown sugar, packed	1/2 cup	125 mL

Beat cake mix, eggs, 1/3 cup (75 mL) melted butter and 1/3 cup (75 mL) water in medium bowl on high for about 3 minutes until smooth.

Add fruit. Stir gently until combined. Spread evenly in greased 3 1/2 to 4 quart (3.5 to 4 L) slow cooker.

Combine brown sugar, 2/3 cup (150 mL) reserved juice and remaining butter in small bowl. Carefully add 3/4 cup (175 mL) boiling water. Stir until sugar is dissolved. Slowly pour over batter. Do not stir. Lay double layer of tea towel over slow cooker liner. Cover with lid. Cook on High for 1 1/2 to 2 hours until wooden pick inserted in centre comes out clean. Let stand, uncovered, for 10 minutes. Serves 8.

1 serving: 523 Calories; 22.8 g Total Fat (7.1 g Mono, 3.8 g Poly, 9.7 g Sat); 84 mg Cholesterol; 80 g Carbohydrate; 3 g Fibre; 6 g Protein; 649 mg Sodium

Tropical Fruit Cobbler

A traditional dessert with a mango twist! Coconut-sprinkled, fluffy biscuits top a sweet, fruity sauce. Brown sugar gives the biscuits a nice colour.

Frozen mango pieces, thawed	6 cups	1.5 L
Can of peach pie filling	19 oz.	540 mL
Biscuit mix	2 cups	500 mL
Brown sugar, packed	1/3 cup	75 mL
Medium sweetened coconut, toasted, divided (see Tip, page 146)	1 cup	250 mL

(continued on next page)

Combine mango and pie filling in 3 1/2 to 4 quart (3.5 to 4 L) slow cooker. Cook, covered, on Low for 6 to 8 hours or on High for 3 to 4 hours. Stir.

Combine biscuit mix, brown sugar and 3/4 cup (175 mL) coconut in medium bowl. Make a well in centre. Add 2/3 cup (150 mL) water. Mix until just combined. Drop batter onto fruit mixture, using about 1/4 cup (60 mL) for each mound. Sprinkle with remaining coconut. Cook, covered, on High for about 1 hour until wooden pick inserted in centre comes out clean. Serves 12.

1 serving: 235 Calories; 4.5 g Total Fat (0.2 g Mono, 0.1 g Poly, 2.4 g Sat); 0 mg Cholesterol; 49 g Carbohydrate; 2 g Fibre; 3 g Protein; 295 mg Sodium

Peaches à la Mode

This combination of sweet, syrupy peaches with pound cake and ice cream makes enough to please a crowd—no oven space required!

Cans of sliced peaches (28 oz., 796 mL, each), drained and juice reserved	2	2
Minute tapioca	2 tbsp.	30 mL
Ground cinnamon	1/2 tsp.	2 mL
Frozen pound cake, thawed	10 1/2 oz.	298 g
Butterscotch ripple ice cream	2 1/2 cups	625 mL

Combine first 3 ingredients and 1/2 cup (125 mL) reserved peach juice in 3 1/2 to 4 quart (3.5 to 4 L) slow cooker. Cook, covered, on Low for 3 to 4 hours or on High for 1 1/2 to 2 hours.

Slice pound cake into 10 slices, about 3/4 inch (2 cm) thick. Top each slice with ice cream. Spoon peach mixture over top. Serves 10.

1 serving: 323 Calories; 11.2 g Total Fat (1.8 g Mono, 0.3 g Poly, 6.9 g Sat); 88 mg Cholesterol; 52 g Carbohydrate; 1 g Fibre; 4 g Protein; 184 mg Sodium

Toffee Pudding Cake

This is a soft, sponge-textured butterscotch cake with a tasty toffee layer on the bottom. Serve each slice with vanilla ice cream.

Large eggs	2	2
Package of white cake mix (1 layer size)	1	1
Box of instant butterscotch pudding powder (4-serving size)	1	1
Cooking oil	1/3 cup	75 mL
Toffee bits	1/2 cup	125 mL

Beat first 4 ingredients and 1/2 cup (125 mL) water on high in medium bowl for about 3 minutes until smooth. Pour into greased 8 inch (20 cm) springform pan. Put an even layer (2 to 3 inches, 5 to 7.5 cm, thick) of crumpled foil into bottom of 5 to 7 quart (5 to 7 L) slow cooker (see Tip, page 80). Pour 2 cups (500 mL) boiling water into slow cooker. Place pan on foil, pushing down gently to settle evenly.

Sprinkle toffee bits over top. Lay double layer of tea towel over slow cooker liner. Cover with lid. Cook on High for 2 hours until wooden pick inserted in centre comes out clean. Transfer pan to wire rack. Let stand for 15 minutes. Cuts into 12 wedges.

1 wedge: 325 Calories; 14.7 g Total Fat (5.6 g Mono, 3.6 g Poly, 3.1 g Sat); 43 mg Cholesterol; 46 g Carbohydrate; trace Fibre; 3 g Protein; 461 mg Sodium

Pictured on page 89.

Paré Pointer

She thought a dry dock was a thirsty physician.

Chunky Spiced Applesauce

This fragrant applesauce is delicious whether served hot or cold, and can be paired with gingerbread or sponge cake.

Chopped peeled tart apples (such as Granny Smith)	16 cups	4 L
Granulated sugar	1 cup	250 mL
Ground cinnamon	1 1/2 tsp.	7 mL
Ground nutmeg	1/2 tsp.	2 mL
Dark raisins (optional)	1/2 cup	125 mL

Combine first 4 ingredients in 5 to 7 quart (5 to 7 L) slow cooker. Pour 1 cup (250 mL) water over top. Cook, covered, on Low for 4 hours or on High for 2 hours.

Add raisins. Stir. Cook, covered, on High for about 1 hour. Stir to break up apples. Makes about 8 cups (2 L).

1/2 cup (125 mL): 131 Calories; 0.2 g Total Fat (trace Mono, 0.1 g Poly, 0.1 g Sat); 0 mg Cholesterol; 34 g Carbohydrate; 3 g Fibre; trace Protein; 3 mg Sodium

Rhuberry Sauce

This thick, delicious rhubarb and strawberry sauce would be wonderful spooned over cakes, ice cream or even pancakes and waffles.

Chopped fresh (or frozen, thawed) rhubarb	6 cups	1.5 L
Container of frozen strawberries in light syrup, thawed	15 oz.	425 g
Granulated sugar	1 cup	250 mL
Minute tapioca	1 tbsp.	15 mL
Cinnamon stick (4 inches, 10 cm)	1	1

Combine all 5 ingredients in 3 1/2 to 4 quart (3.5 to 4 L) slow cooker. Cook, covered, on Low for 5 to 6 hours or on High for 2 1/2 to 3 hours. Remove and discard cinnamon stick. Makes about 5 cups (1.25 L).

1/2 cup (125 mL): 130 Calories; 0.2 g Total Fat (trace Mono, 0.1 g Poly, trace Sat); 0 mg Cholesterol; 33 g Carbohydrate; 2 g Fibre; 1 g Protein; 3 mg Sodium

Coconut Rice Pudding

Creamy and comforting, sweet coconut rice contrasts with the vibrant colour of fresh mango. This is an easy dessert to accompany a Thai or Vietnamese dinner.

Short-grain white rice	2 cups	500 mL
Granulated sugar	1 cup	250 mL
Can of coconut milk	14 oz.	398 mL
Chopped ripe (or frozen, thawed) mango	1 1/2 cups	375 mL
Medium sweetened coconut, toasted (see Tip, page 146)	1/2 cup	125 mL

Put water into large bowl. Add water until rice is covered. Let stand for at least 6 hours or overnight. Drain.

Combine sugar and 3 cups (750 mL) water in 3 1/2 to 4 quart (3.5 to 4 L) slow cooker. Add rice and a light sprinkle of salt. Stir. Cook, covered, on Low for 4 hours or on High for 2 hours.

Add coconut milk and mango. Stir.

Sprinkle coconut over individual servings. Makes about 7 cups (1.75 L).

1/2 cup (125 mL): 210 Calories; 7.1 g Total Fat (0.3 g Mono, 0.1 g Poly, 6.2 g Sat); 0 mg Cholesterol; 36 g Carbohydrate; 1 g Fibre; 2 g Protein; 32 mg Sodium

1. Danish Rice Pudding, page 137
2. Maple Orange Pears, page 148
3. Chocolate Hazelnut Cheesecake, page 147

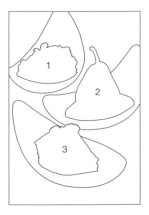

Orange Tapioca Pudding

This citrus-scented tapioca makes for rich and creamy comfort food when served warm, but it can be served up chilled as well.

Seed tapioca	1/2 cup	125 mL
Homogenized milk	3 cups	750 mL
Medium orange	1	1
Large egg	1	1
Granulated sugar	1/3 cup	75 mL

Combine tapioca and 2 cups (500 mL) cold water in medium bowl. Stir. Let stand, covered, for 1 hour. Drain. Transfer to 3 1/2 to 4 quart (3.5 to 4 L) slow cooker.

Add milk and a sprinkle of salt. Stir. Cook, covered, on Low for 4 hours or on High for 2 hours, stirring once at halftime.

Grate 1/2 tsp. (2 mL) orange zest into small bowl. Set aside. Squeeze 1/3 cup (75 mL) orange juice into separate medium bowl.

Add egg and sugar to orange juice. Whisk until smooth. Slowly add about 1 cup (250 mL) hot tapioca mixture, whisking constantly until combined. Slowly add mixture back to slow cooker, stirring constantly. Cook, covered, on High for 15 minutes. Add orange zest. Stir. Makes about 3 1/2 cups (875 mL).

1/2 cup (125 mL): 155 Calories; 4.1 g Total Fat (1.1 g Mono, 0.2 g Poly, 2.4 g Sat); 46 mg Cholesterol; 26 g Carbohydrate; trace Fibre; 4 g Protein; 146 mg Sodium

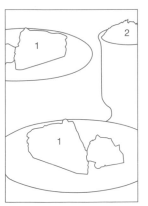

1. Chocolate PB Brownies, page 150
2. Chocolate Peanut Delight, page 31

Saucy Brandied Apples

These aromatic stewed apples feature tart cranberries, sweet raisins and crunchy nuts—a great choice for a winter dessert when your oven is occupied! Serve with a scoop of vanilla ice cream or a dollop of whipped cream.

Brandy	1/2 cup	125 mL
Dried cranberries	1/2 cup	125 mL
Canned raisin pie filling	1 cup	250 mL
Peeled tart apples (such as Granny Smith)	6	6
Chopped pecans, toasted (see Tip, below)	1/4 cup	60 mL

Combine brandy and cranberries in small bowl. Let stand for 15 minutes.

Add pie filling. Stir. Transfer to 5 to 7 quart (5 to 7 L) slow cooker.

Cut apples in half. Remove cores (see Note). Arrange apples, cut-side up, in slow cooker. Cook, covered, on Low for 6 to 7 hours or on High for 3 to 3 1/2 hours. Transfer fruit to large serving plate with slotted spoon. Makes about 1 cup (250 mL) sauce.

Sprinkle apples with pecans. Serve with sauce. Serves 12.

1 serving with 1 tbsp (15 mL) sauce: 111 Calories; 1.9 g Total Fat (1.0 g Mono, 0.6 g Poly, 0.2 g Sat); 0 mg Cholesterol; 18 g Carbohydrate; 2 g Fibre; trace Protein; 17 mg Sodium

Note: A melon baller is a very handy tool for coring an apple that is already peeled and halved

 tip When toasting nuts, seeds or coconut, cooking times will vary for each type of nut—so never toast them together. For small amounts, place ingredient in an ungreased shallow frying pan. Heat on medium for 3 to 5 minutes, stirring often, until golden. For larger amounts, spread ingredient evenly in an ungreased shallow pan. Bake in a 350°F (175°C) oven for 5 to 10 minutes, stirring or shaking often, until golden.

Chocolate Hazelnut Cheesecake

This chocolatey cheesecake has rich flavour but a light texture—delicious!
Top each slice with whipped cream and garnish with fresh berries.

Cream-filled chocolate cookies	10	10
Blocks of cream cheese (8 oz., 250 g, each), softened	2	2
Chocolate hazelnut spread, divided	1 1/3 cups	325 mL
Large eggs, fork-beaten	3	3
Sour cream	1 cup	250 mL

Process cookies in food processor until coarse crumbs form. Press firmly in parchment paper-lined greased 8 inch (20 cm) springform pan. Let stand in freezer for 10 minutes.

Beat cream cheese and 1 cup (250 mL) chocolate hazelnut spread in large bowl, scraping down sides as necessary, until smooth.

Add eggs and sour cream. Beat well. Spread evenly over cookie crumbs. Put an even layer (2 to 3 inches, 5 to 7.5 cm, thick) of crumpled foil into bottom of 5 to 7 quart (5 to 7 L) slow cooker. Pour 2 cups (500 mL) boiling water into slow cooker. Place pan on foil, pushing down gently to settle evenly. Lay double layer of tea towel over slow cooker liner. Cover with lid. Cook on High for 1 1/2 hours. Transfer pan to wire rack. Cool completely. Chill, covered, for at least 6 hours or overnight. Remove from pan. Spread remaining chocolate hazelnut spread over top and sides of cheesecake. Cuts into 12 wedges.

1 wedge: 361 Calories; 26.3 g Total Fat (4.1 g Mono, 1.7 g Poly, 13.3 g Sat); 105 mg Cholesterol; 24 g Carbohydrate; 2 g Fibre; 6 g Protein; 185 mg Sodium

Pictured on page 143.

Paré Pointer

He has no temperature this morning - his mother took it last night.

Buttery Ginger Pineapple

This light dessert is simple yet exotic, with tangy bites of pineapple, buttery sauce with spicy ginger, and a sprinkling of toasted coconut.

Fresh (or frozen, thawed) pineapple chunks (1 1/2 inch, 3.8 cm, pieces)	6 cups	1.5 L
Ginger marmalade	1/4 cup	60 mL
Butter	3 tbsp.	50 mL
Cornstarch	1 tbsp.	15 mL
Flaked coconut, toasted (see Tip, page 146)	1/2 cup	125 mL

Put pineapple into 3 1/2 to 4 quart (3.5 to 4 L) slow cooker.

Combine marmalade and butter in small saucepan on medium-low. Heat and stir until butter is melted. Pour over pineapple. Stir until coated. Cook, covered, on Low for 3 to 4 hours or on High for 1 1/2 to 2 hours.

Stir 1 tbsp. (15 mL) water into cornstarch in small cup until smooth. Add to pineapple. Stir. Cook, covered, on High for 15 minutes until boiling and thickened.

Sprinkle individual servings with coconut. Makes about 4 cups (1 L).

1/2 cup (125 mL): 144 Calories; 5.9 g Total Fat (1.2 g Mono, 0.2 g Poly, 4.0 g Sat); 11 mg Cholesterol; 24 g Carbohydrate; 2 g Fibre; 1 g Protein; 49 mg Sodium

Maple Orange Pears

These tender, golden pears make an elegant yet simple dessert when drizzled with their delicate buttery sauce. Serve with vanilla ice cream for a dinner party.

Maple syrup	1/2 cup	125 mL
Butter (or hard margarine), melted	2 tbsp.	30 mL
Medium firm peeled pears	6	6
Orange juice	2 tbsp.	30 mL
Cornstarch	2 tsp.	10 mL

(continued on next page)

Combine maple syrup, melted butter and 2 tbsp. (30 mL) water in 4 to 5 quart (4 to 5 L) slow cooker.

Carefully remove cores from bottom of pears using apple corer, leaving stems intact. Set upright in maple syrup mixture. Cook, covered, on High for 2 hours. Transfer pears with slotted spoon to serving plate.

Stir orange juice into cornstarch in small cup until smooth. Add to cooking liquid. Stir. Cook, covered, on High for about 20 minutes until thickened. Pour over pears. Serves 6.

1 serving: 205 Calories; 4.1 g Total Fat (1.0 g Mono, 0.2 g Poly, 2.4 g Sat); 10 mg Cholesterol; 45 g Carbohydrate; 5 g Fibre; 1 g Protein; 31 mg Sodium

Pictured on page 143.

Strawberries and Dumplings

Tender dumplings top scrumptious strawberries, all with a hint of lemon—like strawberry shortcake with a twist. Drizzle each serving with a bit of cream.

Small lemon	1	1
Frozen whole strawberries, thawed	4 cups	1 L
Granulated sugar, divided	1/2 cup	125 mL
Biscuit mix	1 cup	250 mL
Milk	1/3 cup	75 mL

Grate 1 tsp. (5 mL) lemon zest into small bowl. Set aside. Squeeze 1 tsp. (5 mL) lemon juice into 3 1/2 to 4 quart (3.5 to 4 L) slow cooker.

Add strawberries and 6 tbsp. (100 mL) sugar to slow cooker. Stir. Cook, covered, on Low for 4 to 5 hours or on High for 2 to 2 1/2 hours until boiling.

Add biscuit mix and remaining sugar to reserved zest. Stir. Add milk. Stir until just moistened. Drop evenly over strawberry mixture in 6 mounds. Cook, covered, on High for about 30 minutes until wooden pick inserted in centre comes out clean. Serves 6.

1 serving: 282 Calories; 2.7 g Total Fat (0.1 g Mono, 0.1 g Poly, 0.6 g Sat); 1 mg Cholesterol; 66 g Carbohydrate; 3 g Fibre; 3 g Protein; 277 mg Sodium

Chocolate PB Brownies

Pour yourself a nice cold glass of milk to go with these delicious chocolate brownies. They would look especially appetizing served with a scoop of vanilla ice cream, drizzled with chocolate sauce and sprinkled with peanuts.

Semi-sweet chocolate baking squares (1 oz., 28 g, each), chopped	5	5
Sweetened condensed milk (see Note)	2/3 cup	150 mL
Crunchy peanut butter	1/2 cup	125 mL
Large egg, fork-beaten	1	1
Biscuit mix	3/4 cup	175 mL

Heat chocolate in medium heavy saucepan on lowest heat, stirring often, until chocolate is almost melted. Remove from heat. Stir until smooth. Transfer to medium bowl.

Add condensed milk. Stir until smooth. Add peanut butter and egg. Stir until combined.

Add biscuit mix. Stir until no dry mix remains. Spread evenly in parchment paper-lined greased 8 inch (20 cm) round cake pan. Put an even layer (2 to 3 inches, 5 to 7.5 cm, thick) of crumpled foil into bottom of 5 to 7 quart (5 to 7 L) slow cooker (see Tip, page 80). Pour 2 cups (500 mL) boiling water into slow cooker. Place pan on foil, pushing down gently to settle evenly. Lay double layer of tea towel over slow cooker liner. Cover with lid. Cook on High for 1 1/2 hours. Transfer pan to wire rack. Let stand for 10 minutes. Cuts into 12 wedges.

1 wedge: 207 Calories; 9.8 g Total Fat (0.6 g Mono, 0.1 g Poly, 3.2 g Sat); 22 mg Cholesterol; 26 g Carbohydrate; 1 g Fibre; 6 g Protein; 170 mg Sodium

Pictured on page 144.

Note: Store remaining sweetened condensed milk in the fridge and use it as a decadent addition to your morning coffee.

Measurement Tables

Throughout this book measurements are given in Conventional and Metric measure. To compensate for differences between the two measurements due to rounding, a full metric measure is not always used. The cup used is the standard 8 fluid ounce. Temperature is given in degrees Fahrenheit and Celsius. Baking pan measurements are in inches and centimetres as well as quarts and litres. An exact metric conversion is given below as well as the working equivalent (Metric Standard Measure).

Spoons

Conventional Measure	Metric Exact Conversion Millilitre (mL)	Metric Standard Measure Millilitre (mL)
1/8 teaspoon (tsp.)	0.6 mL	0.5 mL
1/4 teaspoon (tsp.)	1.2 mL	1 mL
1/2 teaspoon (tsp.)	2.4 mL	2 mL
1 teaspoon (tsp.)	4.7 mL	5 mL
2 teaspoons (tsp.)	9.4 mL	10 mL
1 tablespoon (tbsp.)	14.2 mL	15 mL

Cups

Conventional Measure	Metric Exact Conversion Millilitre (mL)	Metric Standard Measure Millilitre (mL)
1/4 cup (4 tbsp.)	56.8 mL	60 mL
1/3 cup (5 1/3 tbsp.)	75.6 mL	75 mL
1/2 cup (8 tbsp.)	113.7 mL	125 mL
2/3 cup (10 2/3 tbsp.)	151.2 mL	150 mL
3/4 cup (12 tbsp.)	170.5 mL	175 mL
1 cup (16 tbsp.)	227.3 mL	250 mL
4 1/2 cups	1022.9 mL	1000 mL (1 L)

Dry Measurements

Conventional Measure Ounces (oz.)	Metric Exact Conversion Grams (g)	Metric Standard Measure Grams (g)
1 oz.	28.3 g	28 g
2 oz.	56.7 g	57 g
3 oz.	85.0 g	85 g
4 oz.	113.4 g	125 g
5 oz.	141.7 g	140 g
6 oz.	170.1 g	170 g
7 oz.	198.4 g	200 g
8 oz.	226.8 g	250 g
16 oz.	453.6 g	500 g
32 oz.	907.2 g	1000 g (1 kg)

Oven Temperatures

Fahrenheit (°F)	Celsius (°C)
175°	80°
200°	95°
225°	110°
250°	120°
275°	140°
300°	150°
325°	160°
350°	175°
375°	190°
400°	205°
425°	220°
450°	230°
475°	240°
500°	260°

Pans

Conventional Inches	Metric Centimetres
8x8 inch	20x20 cm
9x9 inch	22x22 cm
9x13 inch	22x33 cm
10x15 inch	25x38 cm
11x17 inch	28x43 cm
8x2 inch round	20x5 cm
9x2 inch round	22x5 cm
10x4 1/2 inch tube	25x11 cm
8x4x3 inch loaf	20x10x7.5 cm
9x5x3 inch loaf	22x12.5x7.5 cm

Casseroles

CANADA & BRITAIN		UNITED STATES	
Standard Size Casserole	Exact Metric Measure	Standard Size Casserole	Exact Metric Measure
1 qt. (5 cups)	1.13 L	1 qt. (4 cups)	900 mL
1 1/2 qts. (7 1/2 cups)	1.69 L	1 1/2 qts. (6 cups)	1.35 L
2 qts. (10 cups)	2.25 L	2 qts. (8 cups)	1.8 L
2 1/2 qts. (12 1/2 cups)	2.81 L	2 1/2 qts. (10 cups)	2.25 L
3 qts. (15 cups)	3.38 L	3 qts. (12 cups)	2.7 L
4 qts. (20 cups)	4.5 L	4 qts. (16 cups)	3.6 L
5 qts. (25 cups)	5.63 L	5 qts. (20 cups)	4.5 L

Recipe Index

152

153

154

Q

R

Celebrating the
Harvest
RECIPES FOR FALL & WINTER GATHERINGS

Whether from the garden, farmers' market or supermarket, harvest ingredients display the bounty and beauty of nature. Entertain a crowd in style, or feed your family comfort food they'll not soon forget—with new delicious recipes that celebrate harvest ingredients. What a lovely way to get through the long fall and winter!

If you like what we've done with **cooking**, you'll **love** what we do with **crafts**!